Welcome to Cork Golf Club, Ireland, for the 2010 MacKenzie Tournament, to be played on August 22nd, 23rd and 24th. As a long-time member of Cork Golf Club, I am delighted to present you with a complementary copy of my book, "Lazy Days in Lahinch", as a memento of the occasion. This book was inspired by summer holiday golf at that other great Irish MacKenzie course, Lahinch, Co. Clare, in the 1970's.

Yours sincerely,

G. A. Finn - Author

Further stories about golf and golfers, and those who have to live with them, can be found on my website:

WWW.THELAHINCHCHRONICLES.COM.

Lazy Days at Lahinch

———

by

G.A. Finn

Sleeping Bear Press

Originally published as *Through the Green, Lightly,* Golfinn Publications, Ltd., Ireland, 1997.

These stories are figments of the author's imagination. They are set in Lahinch, County Clare, Ireland, for verisimilitude, as one might set a murder mystery in London, Dublin or Cork. The characters and incidents portrayed are all fictional and do not in any way refer to anyone, living or dead, connected with Lahinch Golf Club, or Lahinch village, or the surrounding area, or any golf club of which the author has been a member or an employee. Some liberties have been taken with the physical layout of both the village and the Links to emphasize the fictional nature of these stories. Any similarity to any living person or real event is entirely coincidental.

Sleeping Bear Press
310 North Main Street
P.O. Box 20
Chelsea, MI 48118
www.sleepingbearpress.com

Printed and bound in Canada.

10 9 8 7 6 5 4 3 2 1

Library of Congress Cataloging-in-Publication Data

Finn, G. A.
 Lazy days at Lahinch / by G.A. Finn.
   p. cm.
 ISBN 1-58536-080-5
 1. Lahinch Golf Club (Lahinch, Clare, Ireland)—Anecdotes. I. Title.
 GV969.L35 F56 2002
 796.352'06'84193—dc21

                                                                2001006348

To the girls in my life: my mother, Maisie (RIP),
who started it all; my wife Veronica, who had to
live with it; and my daughter, Deborah,
who didn't understand it at all.

Acknowledgments

My thanks to Gloria Greenwood for her invaluable assistance in preparing the manuscript, and to Batt Murphy for his encouragement. Thanks also to my agent, Jim Donovan, whose sound advice and steady hand keep me on the straight and narrow. Wish he could do the same for me on the golf course!

Table of Contents

ꙮ Funny Old World ꙮ

———

HERE WAS I, recuperating from a car accident, minding my own business, when out of the blue my older sister, under the guise of sibling concern, sent me an advertisement for a job that she had seen in her local paper. To humour her and pass the time, I brought my CV up-to-date, typed it neatly and sent it off, never expecting to hear from Lahinch Golf Club again, and not being overly concerned at that.

My left leg still gave me some pain and I also suffered from intermittent headaches, so I was still taking the medication prescribed by my doctor. The reason that I mention these unsavoury details is that I suspect that the medication had a part to play in the events that took place subsequently. I'm sure that my CV was no better than the others they received, and, to be honest, I was not even particularly interested in the position. However, my degree from UCC and a bit of experience in retail management, plus my previous connection with the game itself, prompted the subcommittee to offer me an interview.

As they had very kindly included an offer "to contribute to the expenses of those travelling long distances and who may have to stay overnight," I dashed off a note advising said gentlemen that I looked forward to meeting them on the day specified. I considered that, if nothing came of it, I would at least have had a pleasant day by the sea and an overnight stay in a hotel, which would undoubtedly be more congenial than my present accommodation, with which I was becoming quite fed up.

The evening before my departure I packed an overnight bag, borrowed a second alarm clock from a friend to ensure that there would be no problem in the waking-up department next morning, and read a few chapters of a novel. I packed myself off to bed early, with just the slightest buzz of anticipation, as evidenced by the fact that I forgot to take my sleeping tablet. Some time later I realised that nothing was happening on the sleep front, so I had to rectify the omission, with much groping in the dark and banging of bottles and glasses.

I have only the vaguest recollection of the journey, which was partly by train and partly by bus. The latter I found very uncomfortable, in my still fragile condition, and it put me off that mode of transport for life. I increased the dosage of medication to ease the pain and discomfort. It seems that when I had lunch in the Aberdeen Arms Hotel in Lahinch, my aperitif consisted of a large gin and tonic. In hindsight, this choice may have been unwise. The interaction between the aperitif and the tablets rendered me immune to the sensitivities of others and put me in high good humour, a deadly combination.

The walk to the Golf Club from the hotel cleared my head somewhat, so that the early part of the interview went quite well. It was not until I was tiring a little from the effort of concentrating that one of the older members of the interview board asked what was obviously a trick question, and I slipped my gears.

"I would like to get your opinion on a hypothetical situation," he started off innocuously. "Imagine that one of our more prominent members was dining here and, between an appetiser beforehand, a bottle of good claret with his meal, and a little something to aid the digestion afterward, he was feeling ever so slightly merry, and this caused a slight, er, shall we say, indiscretion on his part, involving one of the young waitresses in the dining room. The Committee feels that this kind of thing could not be overlooked in this day and age, and yet would not wish to give unnecessary embarrassment to a distinguished member of the Club, who may have given many years of valuable service. If you, as Secretary/Manager, were to advise the Captain on such a matter, how would you suggest he handle it?"

What I did not know until later was that this gentleman favoured another candidate for the position and that this sidewinder of a question was designed to either throw me off balance altogether or to put me in a no-win situation, where whatever answer I gave could be construed as wrong.

A deathly hush descended on the room, or so it seemed to me, and my concentration deepened to hitherto unknown depths for several seconds. From somewhere deep inside my head, a thought slowly emerged.

"The young lady in question should be given an immediate pay rise for her hard work and loyalty to the Club. And the offending member should be banned from the Snooker Room for one month."

In the silence that followed this inspired judgment, a number of reactions showed on the faces around the table. There was one definite grin, quickly covered with a hand. Another could have been either admiration for the dexterity of my thinking or amazement at my stupidity. A loud cough and a look of disapproval from another. And, ominously, a gleam of triumph in the eye of the questioner.

"But, sir," he oozed icily, "we do not have a Snooker Room." Momentarily fazed by this devastating piece of information, my befuddled brain gave up the hopeless task of trying to find an intelligent solution to my dilemma and I delivered myself as follows:

"Then ban the blighter for three months!"

Such a response would normally be the death knell to anyone's aspirations for a job. But the Lord moves in mysterious ways. At the end of the day there was deadlock over the choice of candidate, with the subcommittee split two ways. I learned long afterward, when I had become part of the furniture at Lahinch, that I was offered the job as a compromise candidate, because, the Chairman claimed, "Only someone with a sense of humour could possibly survive as Manager of a golf club!"

☙ THE ROAD TO DAMASCUS ☙

"AND MAY HIS soul rest in peace, Amen," intoned the Bishop, as the last mortal remains of Canon Jeremiah O'Connor, Parish Priest of Lahinch and Liscannor, were laid to rest in the gray October graveyard.

The crowd dispersed and the visiting dignitaries made their way to the presbytery for tea and sandwiches (or something a little stronger for those who wanted it) before returning to their respective homes. When the last of the mourners had left, Father Malachy Murphy, curate of that same parish, sat deep in thought, the golden liquid in the cut crystal glass in his hand forgotten. Who would succeed Canon O'Connor?

He considered in depth the snatches of clerical conversations that he had assiduously overheard and retained throughout the day for any clue as to the identity of his new boss. Several names had been bandied about, but nothing definite. He was quite sure that he would not get the job himself, as he needed much more experience before ever contemplating such a promotion, but this did not bother him. He was not a particularly ambitious man, being quite content to minister to his flock under the supervision of a more senior cleric. As long as the man played golf!

He contemplated the havoc that could be wreaked on his life by an uncomprehending nongolfer. He could just imagine the remarks even now, should the "wrong" man be appointed:

"It's only a game, Fr. Malachy."

"Duty calls, Fr. Malachy."

"You must put yourself in God's hands, Fr. Malachy."

"The Good Shepherd always puts his flock first, Fr. Malachy."

Fluck the flock, thought Fr. Malachy irreverently to himself. *Please God, let him be a golfer. Even a beginner would do. I'd go demented without the odd game.*

The "odd game" in Fr. Malachy's book consisted of both Saturday mornings and Sunday afternoons, frequent Wednesdays, and many balmy evenings during the long summer, deaths, births, marriages (and visits by the Bishop) permitting. He dropped to his knees from the chair and prayed mightily for a miracle. But it was not to be. Monsignor Pius Ignatious O'Flaherty was no golfer. But he was the new PP of Lahinch and Liscannor.

The news was broken to Fr. Malachy the following Saturday night after the Golfers' Mass at 7:00 p.m. in Lahinch, by means of a phone call from the Bishop's Secretary at the Diocesan Office in Ennis. Fr. Malachy was shattered. He jumped into his car and drove immediately to the doctor's house at the other end of the village.

"Jasus, Joseph, I'm shagged," he blurted out as Doctor Joe Moore opened the front door.

"What's the matter, man. Come in out of the cold and tell me all about it. What are you shagged over?"

Fr. Malachy took a quick sip of the two fingers of Jameson whiskey that the good doctor had instantly prescribed, knowing full well that this was the best treatment for someone in the kind of shock from which the young curate was suffering.

"Now calm down and tell me all about it."

"I've just heard from Ennis. The new PP is a Monsignor Pius Ignatious O'Flaherty. A studious, saintly man, a former President of the Seminary, I'm told, but not a golfer. Books, bridge, and a passion for public speaking are the loves of his life. Apart from Holy Mother Church, of course. What in the name of God am I to do?"

Dr. Moore understood his predicament precisely. He thought about it for a moment and then said, "Mal, there's nothing can be done for now. Let's meet the good Monsignor and see how he shapes up. You might be worrying about nothing at all. Drink up now and tell me how an auld bandit like you picked up another turkey in last week's competition. Have you no shame?"

Fr. Malachy allowed himself to be distracted and they chatted on about the winnings and losings at the Club for a while, until he had calmed down enough to make his way home. He said an extra decade of the Rosary that night at the side of his bed before he retired to sleep, that the Good Lord would support him on the hard road ahead.

At first the Good Lord appeared to ignore this plea, for the way ahead in the following months was very hard on Fr. Malachy. The concept of "day off" went out the window. Any time off that he did get was of such a fragmented nature that there was no way a round of golf could be fitted into it. It was impossible to plan ahead, golfwise, that is, and he figured that his spiritual handicap must now be in Category 1 whilst his golf handicap was heading rapidly for Category 3. He would prefer it the other way round, although he could never admit that aloud.

Worse was to follow. The "Mons," as he was called, announced that there would be a fortnight's Spring Mission in the parish in the New Year, an event that had not taken place too often in the recent past.

A Mission for two weeks meant that he would be tied up for the best part of a month, with the preparations beforehand and the tidying up afterward. Was there no end to it? The summer would be upon him before he managed to get his game into any sort of shape at all, if he ever did again. All the clerical cowboys from around the country who regularly holidayed in Lahinch each year would start arriving soon. They provided Fr. Malachy with a tidy supplement to his modest income in the form of small bets on the many rounds of golf he felt compelled, as the "host" curate, to play with them. And here he was, still shooting in the mid-80s, whenever he could get in a round! He could be cleaned out or else—perish the thought—he'd have to give up playing with them altogether.

He turned to Dr. Joe for consolation again.

"What am I going to do, Joe?" he asked in exasperation. "The man is a slave driver."

"I'll tell you what, Mal. Why don't you set up a bit of a dinner some evening next week and invite me and another bridge player. To get to know the Monsignor, so to speak. It's time to beard the lion in his den, methinks."

The dinner was duly arranged for Fr. Malachy's house, with Mrs. Casey from the Club drafted in to do the catering, and another bridge player was recruited. The Monsignor's fondness for a hand or two of this particular card game of an evening had preceded him.

After a very satisfying meal, accompanied by a rather special claret from P.J. Egan's in Liscannor that the Doctor had taken particular care to acquire for the occasion, they retired to the sitting room and proceeded to play a few hands. The wine and the good company, for everyone had been primed to be on their very best behaviour, gradually led to the easing of the starch in the Monsignor's collar and he began to enjoy the evening. Tom O'Rourke, a retired engineer now resident in Lahinch, and a very fine bridge player indeed, asked, as he conceded an easy trick, "And how is it, Monsignor, that you never got around to playing the noble game of golf?"

"Never really had the time for it, Tom. Although I must admit that it is a game that appears particularly pointless, hitting a little white ball around a field with implements ill designed for the purpose."

"Well," said the Doctor quickly, before anyone overreacted to this appalling heresy, "it does have definite beneficial effects, both physical and psychological. I only wish more of my patients played it, for the sake of their health."

Fr. Malachy got a smart tap on the shin from the good doctor so that he would say nothing out of turn. He gazed in amazement, as the man blatantly disregarded the fact that 90% of his patients did play golf, the links being the most likely place to find him for a consultation.

"Indeed, indeed," demurred the Monsignor, "how very facetious of me. Of course it must be a splendid game for so many to be so devoted to it."

"Of course," went on Dr. Joe, "it probably would not have the intellectual challenge that a man of your training and capacity would require."

"Oh, I wouldn't say that, Doctor. I swung a mean hurling stick in my youth and, I must say, I enjoyed the recreational aspects of the game very much."

"Still, with your analytical ability, your experience of decision making, your evident self-control, the mental and moral discipline you are used to, it probably would not be much of a challenge. I could see you mastering that old course in a year or two, once you got the hang of the basic rules and so forth."

The conspiring company nodded in approval and Tom slipped in another little dart, "Wouldn't surprise me if they started bothering you to become President after a while, if you ever got involved in the game. That could be a bit of a nuisance. Speeches and all that."

The Monsignor's fondness for learned but lengthy sermons had been noted in the village already. He preened slightly as he took another easy trick from Tom.

"Hmmm, certain civic duties are not altogether unpleasant, although they do tend to eat into one's time."

They let the hare sit at that and played a few more hands before yawning suggestively.

"Well, I must hit the sack, Monsignor," said the Doctor, "I have a big operation early in the morning. Thank you, Fr. Malachy, for a most enjoyable evening."

He omitted to say that the kind of "operation" he had in mind took place on a golf links and involved two, or even three, equally addicted practitioners of the Royal and Ancient Game.

A short while after the little dinner-cum-bridge party for Pius Ignatious, on a nice mild spring day, the aforementioned cleric took himself off to a discreet little nine-hole golf course in the seaside town of Kilkee, some 45 minutes driving time from his home parish, where he intended to conduct a little experiment away from any prying eyes that might disturb his concentration. Carefully leaving aside anything that might be indicative of his high clerical office, he made his way onto the course, hired a dilapidated set of clubs and prudently purchased six second-hand golf balls. Two hours later he handed back the clubs, put the one remaining ball in his pocket and retired to the small bar for some light refreshment. Reviewing the events of the afternoon, while munching on a particularly tasty ham sandwich and sipping a glass of cold beer that had his taste buds tingling, he reluctantly concluded that the experiment had not been entirely successful.

True, he had a fine appreciation of the necessary tactics to minimise risk and maximise one's chances of obtaining one of those quaintly named "pars" at any particular hole. He was an excellent judge of distance, rapidly realising which of the rented rusty relics would propel the ball any given number of yards. But the control of the direction in which the ball travelled eluded him.

He mulled over the problem while he polished off his snack and then, slightly dispirited, he returned to his car and resumed his former persona. As he sat into it and slammed the door with just a hint of annoyance, the car's instruction manual popped out of the side pocket onto the floor and he had to reach down to retrieve it. As he read the words "Instruction Manual" emblazoned in large gold letters on the front cover of the booklet, he had a flash of inspiration that could almost be termed "divine." He needed to establish how to hit the ball straight before he could learn to do it properly!

He turned the key in the ignition with a light heart, revved the engine joyously and, not unlike St. Peter, set off toward Limerick City on what was his second major mistake of the day. As he drove along the twisting road he hummed to himself, blissfully unaware that he was moving inexorably toward his third and fatal error.

In the finest bookshop on O'Connell Street, he strode purposefully up to a sales attendant and said, "I'm interested in looking at some instruction booklets on golf. Do you have anything in stock?"

Young George O'Brien looked up at the middle-aged cleric. George was a five-handicap golfer at the nearby Castletroy Golf Club and knew his game quite well. The right man in the right place with the right solution to a problem. A dozen different assistants in a dozen different bookshops could have handed him a dozen different books. But young O'Brien handed him, without hesitation, Ben Hogan's *Five Lessons, The Modern Fundamentals of Golf,* written in conjunction with Herbert Warren Wind and illustrated brilliantly by Anthony Ravielli. This classic instruction book became, not only Pius Ignatious's bible (in the strictly golfing sense, of course), but the foundation of what would grow to become one of the finest collections of golf books in the entire province and exceeded on the island of Ireland only by one other, in the southerly city of Cork.

Pius Ignatious never became much of a golfer himself, but he did gain a great understanding of the breed, and Fr. Malachy's life became bearable again. The Monsignor could talk a great game with the best of them and he peppered his speeches with erudite references to, and quotations from, the great and the good of the game, when he was called upon to speak, as he frequently was in his capacity as President of Lahinch Golf Club, to which exalted office he was elected some three years after his "conversion."

↫ The Price of Perfection ↬

THERE ARE TWO great gifts in this miserable life, a perfect putter
and a perfect wife. Some get one, as a great favour, but most
have to struggle without one or the other. A privileged few, upon
my oath, sail through this life blessed with both. Roly Monaghan
was one of these.

His wife, Lucy, was a petite beauty, with dark hair and pearly
white teeth. After two children she still had a great figure and
dressed, on a very modest budget, with excellent taste. She was
utterly supportive of her man in his work and in his golf and
never nagged. They lived happily in a neat bungalow on the
Lahinch side of Ennistymon.

His putter was a very old model, hickory shafted and hand
forged long before modern technology was brought to bear on
the making of golf clubs. With a worn grip and a head with rust
spots, it would, perhaps, have been more at home in a museum.
Somehow or other, the craftsman who had made this putter had

got the balance perfect and, just as Excalibur had to await Arthur's coming, so this putter was a nonentity until Roly took it in his hands one day in a junk shop, felt good about it and purchased it for one pound and 10 shillings. The rest is history. Number one on the Lahinch Senior Cup Team, which went to the National Finals in Portmarnock; a regular on the Munster Interprovincial Team for several years; umpteen Senior Scratch Cups up and down the country; and international honours just around the corner. The man had everything.

Such men have a fatal attraction for a certain kind of woman, one who wants to pit her charms against all that he has going for him. Shirley Brighthopp was such a girl. A woman of the world, she had been married once, briefly, but only to see what it was like. She became bored with living with the same man all the time. She craved new challenges. She wanted Roly Monaghan.

One would have thought that a man with Roly's gifts would have been impervious to the charms of such a woman. But she was clever. She never praised him. She blew hot and then, just when he began to enjoy it, she went cold again. She was always about when he was playing and winning, especially when Lucy had to stay at home to mind the children. She made herself available to him, but only up to a point. She flirted and teased unmercifully for a time, and then went distant and silent. Like any man, he was flattered by her attentions when she bestowed them and began to miss them when she withdrew them. He made several passes at her, especially after a few celebratory drinks, but she made sure nothing came of them. She was after higher stakes.

Lucy was uneasily aware that something was going on, but there was never anything definite to latch onto. Friends issued warnings that she laughed off in public, but which concerned her greatly in private. She did everything a good wife and mother should do for her man and her family, but to no avail. She was no match for Shirley Brighthopp.

The fall came after Roly won the East of Ireland Strokeplay Championship. His putter worked like a magic wand on the superb greens of the links course at Baltray, County Louth, where this major amateur championship is held every June.

His putting stroke was a wonder to behold. He would take two practice swings, having carefully studied the line of a putt first. Then he stood quite tall over the ball, which he positioned behind the left toe, about six inches away from the body, feet shoulder-width apart to give himself a good solid base. He gripped the club with all the fingers of the right hand, thumb straight down the shaft, with the left forefinger overlapping and only three fingers of the left on the shaft. He used the orthodox interlocking grip with all the other clubs.

He would bring the putter head back very close to the ground, compared to other golfers, and many people maintained that this was the secret of his success. There was no hint of a wrist break, and then the putter swept the ball toward the hole with a beautiful roll that seemed to keep it moving long after it should have run out of steam. Many's the putt of his that dropped into the hole on the last half-roll, much to the chagrin of his opponents. In fact, he got his name "Roly" from this characteristic of his game, his correct name being John Anthony.

The rest of his game was nothing remarkable. Indeed it was deficient in some respects, but nothing that couldn't be corrected with proper tuition and plenty of practice, both of which he was getting. This, his first amateur "major," was proof that it was all paying off. A good, reliable putting stroke is a gift and, while certain aspects of it can be taught, nothing can beat the naturally gifted putter. And no one did that weekend. Except himself, after the golf was over, with Shirley Brighthopp.

Lucy found out, of course, just as the bold Shirley had intended, and she was devastated. Once she realised that everybody knew, her pride would not allow her to stay in the same house as Roly. So one day shortly afterward, while he was at work basking in the adulation of his colleagues, she packed her bags, put the two children in the back of the car and started the engine. Then she turned it off again, warned the children to behave themselves, went back into the house and took his putter out of his golf bag and departed. On the way to her mother's house in Limerick, she stopped the car on a bridge near Bunratty Castle, took the putter and dropped it into the back of a passing grain lorry on the highway below. It left the country in that lorry and ended up as a walking stick in the hands of an old lady in a village in Turkey.

He laughed it off for a while, but, not being a fool, he soon came to realise what a mistake he had made. He bought a new putter, but it was not the same. He started to miss putts that he would normally have rolled in as a matter of course. He changed his putter again, but to no avail. He lost his place on one team, and then another. He changed putters several times more, but always without success. When his fortunes started going downhill, he was quickly abandoned by his paramour, Shirley, who had by now tired of the game and wanted to move on to pastures new. Altogether over the next few months he changed his putter nine times!

He was a ruined man. He barely held on to his job. The house went to rack and ruin. He became scruffy and unkempt. Eventually, he stopped playing golf. Friends pleaded with Lucy to give the putter back, but she had disposed of it completely and could not return it now even if she wanted to. She heard of his deterioration with a heavy heart and many tears.

After 12 months, when the emotional scars had healed a little, Fr. Malachy, the local curate, effected a reconciliation of sorts. They started talking to each other again. Roly began to visit the children at Lucy's mother's house, where they were now living. The tender shoot of love that had been so callously killed off by the frost of Shirley's breath once again pushed its head, gingerly, above ground. Roly began to pull himself together, little by little. The wounds in Lucy's heart began to heal. Finally, they were fully reconciled. They set off on a second honeymoon, to get things off to a good start, while Lucy's mother looked after the children. They moved up to Limerick to live. Roly pledged himself to Lucy and the children and, in a gesture of good faith, gave up golf forever and took up fishing. Needless to say, he never made the Irish Team.

✥ Balls ✥

"Old Cobblers" was generally reckoned to be one sandwich short of a picnic. The fact that he enjoyed a pint of plain overmuch did nothing to reduce this impression. A total disregard for the effect that his unkind comments might have on his employers completes the picture.

John Joseph Murray, to give him his correct title, was a sometime caddie, golf ball finder, odd-job man and gardener (if you are prepared to allow some latitude in the meaning of that word). Most of all, however, he was a "ward of the State," as he grandiloquently referred to himself from time to time. He could only refer to himself in this manner from time to time, because when he had a few too many taken, which was more than a few times too often, he had great difficulty getting the sounds to come out of his mouth in the correct order. He was, in effect, kept afloat, if you will excuse the pun, by the Social Welfare system.

He came by his nickname from his inconsiderate habit of referring to various golfers' efforts to propel the ball toward the hole as a "load of old cobblers." The fact that his description was quite apt, more often than not, did nothing to soften the blow. On one notable occasion, he described a large American gentleman who applied more brawn than brain to the playing of the game as "built like a bungalow—very big, but with nothing upstairs."

Despite these failings, Old Cobblers had a small (but diminishing) band of supporters. They were all men who were prepared to put up with the vicissitudes of having him for a caddie because occasionally he gave good advice and at other times his remarks were quite priceless. But mostly he was employed out of a sense of charity, and very often the stipend was much more generous than the service provided justified.

He also caused a certain nuisance to the Club, but the cost of solving the problem of his constant trespassing whilst looking for golf balls or trapping rabbits would have been prohibitive. It was hinted that perhaps I might direct my attention toward resolving the problem, shortly after I commenced work in Lahinch, but it was a half-hearted suggestion and early on it became obvious that I would be wasting my time.

Old Cobblers and I soon worked out a "modus vivendi," whereby I would occasionally reprimand him publicly for his various misdemeanors and he would skulk off into the undergrowth, not to appear again for a reasonable time, thus satisfying the "powers that be" that I was sternly enforcing the law. The rest of the time I would leave him in peace to search for his supper (rabbits) or funds for liquid refreshment (golf balls).

One of his less endearing habits was to spend an evening drinking away his money, especially when a good tip by a considerate golfer coincided with payday at the Employment Exchange. After whichever public house had been graced with his presence had finally pried him out the door, he would make his way home by a shortcut across the links.

Invariably, he lacked either the will or the stamina, or both, to complete the journey and picked out an appropriate bunker, allowing for wind direction, slope, depth of sand, and so forth, and bunked down there for the night, so to speak. He would shape the sand into a hollow for his bum and a pillow for his head and sleep off the effects of the night's overindulgence. Mostly this was not a problem, except when there was a competition the next morning and the players would reach the hole before Old Cobblers arose to greet the new day. After this had happened two or three times, I arranged with Dougie McDowell to have the groundsmen on early duty keep a sharp eye out for the recumbent figure and to move him on when located.

One Saturday morning I received a call from the groundsman on duty to say that he had located Old Cobblers but that he seemed to be unable to move, even when quite forcibly requested to do so, and would I mind coming out to have a look at him. Grumbling fierce threats under my breath, I reluctantly agreed and, fearing the worst, I called the Ennistymon Hospital's emergency service to send along an ambulance. We arrived at the offending bunker (this, I believe, may be a literary device known as a "transferred epitaph," where it was the occupant of the bunker that was giving offence, rather than the bunker itself) simultaneously, and there was Old Cobblers in an alcoholic stupor.

The groundsman, who was experienced in these matters, pointed out that Old Cobblers had not been in his usual position when discovered. When I enquired curiously what his normal posture was, he said he usually looked like a hedgehog, all rolled up in a ball, with his old coat pulled over his head.

The ambulance personnel carefully manoeuverd him into an upright position and brought him back to this world by the simple expedient of placing the most foul-smelling substance I have ever come across under his nose. It speaks volumes for Old Cobblers' tolerance of foul smells that it took him all of 10 seconds to respond. Or perhaps he only drew breath at 10-second intervals when inebriated.

He did regain consciousness eventually and promptly let out a loud moan. Further investigation by the dedicated paramedic located the problem in Old Cobblers' left leg, which he quickly established was broken. Exposure overnight had not helped the poor man's condition but, paradoxically, his inebriation had helped, in so far as he was sort of "pickled" for the night and survived somewhat better than he would have had he been sober. After much huffing and puffing, moaning and groaning, the injured man was placed aboard the ambulance and carted off to Ennistymon.

Although the Club had no direct responsibility for Old Cobblers and his predicament, the Captain asked me to keep an eye on him. He said he considered him in the same light as the two old goats that wandered around the Old Course: part of the scenery. So I visited him in the hospital a couple of times, rather briefly I admit, for Old Cobblers was not in the best of humours.

The Matron's aversion to alcoholic drink in her wards and the onset of withdrawal symptoms were taking their toll.

I was told by Dr. Joe Moore that the break was quite severe and that he would probably walk with a limp for the rest of his life. How he would cope with a long recuperation was going to be a major problem. He lived alone and his accommodation was not the most congenial in the world.

A social worker visited the hospital on a regular basis and undertook to look into his case. It transpired that he would be entitled to very limited assistance for the duration of his recuperation outside the hospital. It was also clear that the man could not be trusted to look after himself properly for any length of time. He adamantly refused to go to a State-run nursing home in Ennis. He would have to be looked after locally and it would not be easy to get a volunteer for this task, even if he could afford to pay for it, which he manifestly could not.

We were collectively musing over this problem when it was decided that we should check out his home to ensure that it had not deteriorated in his absence, or that vandals were not up to their dirty work. The Captain, his friend Mrs. Montgomery, and I went over to his cottage one evening after work and had a look inside. It was damp and cold and smelled rather badly.

"He can't stay here, that's for sure," said the Captain.

Mrs. Mon and I agreed and we pondered the problem in silence. Mrs. Mon started to hem and haw a bit then, as if she had something to say but did not quite know how to get it out.

"I have a bit of time on my hands, now that it's the off-season," she said, "and I have room at the house, but I could not possibly afford to keep him on my limited means. I would prob-ably need help with him, too."

There was the glimmer of a solution here, but the financing of the arrangements presented an obstacle. Mrs. Mon was quite right, too. She could not possibly look after such a contrary old man herself and would need qualified help for the duration of the convalescence.

We set about tidying up the place a bit while we mulled over the situation. Mrs. Mon discovered a large trunk tucked away in a corner, covered with all sorts of rubbish and old clothes.

"Would we be out of order looking in this trunk for any-thing he might need?" she asked, looking at it dubiously. The Captain went over and hefted it experimentally with one hand. It was heavy. Easing it back onto the floor, he said, "I'll check with Sergeant Twomey to see if it would be okay to investigate this a little further."

A short while later he was back in the room and reported that the Sergeant himself would be there within minutes. Sure enough, he arrived very quickly and the two of them looked the trunk over. They could see that it was only held closed by a bolt with a small lock on it. When the Sergeant went to test the lock, the whole thing came away in his hand. He carefully eased open the heavy lid. Inside, a dirty black cloth covered the contents. Lifting the corner of this, he gasped.

"Would you look at this," he said in wonder.

We all crowded around the trunk, eagerly trying to get a glimpse of its mysterious contents. Hundreds, if not thousands, of bright, shiny golf balls filled the trunk to the top. Every one of them was secondhand, but in very good condition. The silly old fool had been keeping the best of all the golf balls he had found over the years, storing them as his treasure trove, selling only the inferior ones. This was a timely discovery indeed. The Captain beamed.

"If we can get the old fool to agree to sell this lot to the Pro Shop, it should raise quite a bit of money toward paying for his recuperation. We could, I suppose, run a benefit competition to top it up, too," he smiled, pleased with himself for coming up with a solution.

We covered up the chest and headed off to the hospital to persuade Old Cobblers to part with his shiny white treasure. When the proposition was put to him, he gazed off into the distance, considering the matter. Then, nodding his head in agreement, he muttered under his breath, "Oh, balls."

We never did figure out what he meant.

❧ Banished ❧

"HE'LL HAVE TO GO, Jim, and that's an end to it. I cannot have that sort of thing on my patch," said the Chief Superintendent of the Limerick Metropolitan Area as he slapped the file shut.

"But, Chief," pleaded the Superintendent, "he's got a young family. They're all at school. Can't you give him some 'latrine duty' for a couple of months to teach him a lesson and leave it at that?"

"Sorry, Jim, too many noses out of joint. I mean, two judges, a T.D., the State Solicitor and the President of the Chamber of Commerce! Was the man mad? A warning and a blind eye would have taken care of it. But no, the bold Sergeant had to be a hero! Too much bloody television, if you ask me. He'll have to learn to live in the real world. If we cracked down on after-hours drinking without using our heads, we'd all be shagged. Get the eejit out of my sight before he does any more damage and drags us all down with him."

Superintendent Houlihan saw that it was hopeless. The Chief Superintendent was right. The offending thorn had to be removed from the flesh and deposited as far away as possible. He was not looking forward to the interview.

"Find Sergeant Twomey for me," he said to his Ban Garda secretary when he returned to his own office. Some minutes later the overzealous Sergeant marched smartly into the office and stood to attention.

"Well, Sergeant Twomey, you've really done it this time. I went out on a limb for you, but to no avail. Your transfer will be through in a week. Get yourself organised to leave next Monday."

Tim Twomey was stunned. He hadn't thought it would come to this. He had just wanted to teach the arrogant bastards a lesson. It wasn't fair that he had to pay the piper for their indiscretions!

The kindly Superintendent could see that the man was in shock. He softened his tone.

"Tim, I'm really sorry. But you went too far this time. I'll do all I can to get you back into circulation as quickly as possible, but it will take a few years. At least. It will have to wait for a new Chief, at the earliest. I know that the family is going to be disrupted, but that goes with the turf anyway."

"Is there nothing can be done, sir?" Tim asked.

The Superintendent lowered his head and stared silently at the file. Gathering up his courage, the fearful Sergeant asked, "Where am I going?"

"Lahinch. Dismissed, Sergeant."

Tim Twomey somehow removed himself from the office without crying out. He leaned against the wall of the corridor and closed his eyes tightly.

Lahinch! The mecca of golfers from all over Ireland and I'm going to live there permanently! he thought. There was a God after all and, as far as Sergeant Timothy J. Twomey was concerned, that God was a golfer.

He was breathing easier now. He tried to think. Mustn't be seen to be happy about it. Long face. Head down. Plenty of sniffling. Even the wife must not suspect, though she was cute enough to suss him out unless he was extremely careful. The Ban Garda passed him on her way into the Superintendent's office, and he managed a watery smile.

"How is he taking it?" the Superintendent asked her when she had closed the door.

"Hard, but he seems to be bearing up," she replied.

"Poor sod!" said the Superintendent. "Some people never learn."

"Yes, sir," said the Ban Garda, filing the lesson away in her mind.

Marie Twomey couldn't figure out what was going on in her husband's head. She knew that his career had been dealt a severe blow and yet he seemed to be taking it very well. He was upset, of course, but not as much as that time two years ago when he three-putted the eighteenth green to lose the Captain's Prize at Charleville, where he had to go to play his golf these days.

Well, she thought, as she watched him gazing out of the upstairs window of the white Garda Station in Lahinch that was to be their new home, *at least he won't have so far to travel for his game of golf now.*"

"Cheer up, love, it won't be forever. What are you staring at?"

"Oh, just the seagulls," said Tim, morosely, as he dragged his gaze away from the four-ball making their way down the hill on the second fairway of the famous old links.

"Why don't you have a look around that golf course before you go on duty this afternoon, pet? It'll do you good."

"Yes, dear, I think I will. But it's called a golf 'links,' you know."

She looked at him blankly and snorted. A links? A course? What's the difference?

He shook his head and sighed. Only a *real golfer* would understand!

❧ His Lordship ❧

———

HE IS ONE of the few men that I have ever known who appears to do nothing but is, at the same time, in complete control of everyone and everything in his vicinity. He does little work and is well paid for it, mostly in large, tax-free tips. He has no official authority, but in many ways runs the Club. He has a lowly status in the pecking order, but maintains the most comfortable office on the premises. He owns nothing, but is one of the most powerful men in Lahinch. And he loves a little flutter. I speak of none other than Bob Dickins, the Caddiemaster/Starter.

His position is supported by two great obvious pillars: his power to allocate whatever caddie he chooses to a player, and his control of the time sheets. A third, invisible pillar, namely his willingness to take a bet on practically anything, props up the other two in an unshakeable tripod that ensures that he will have the job for life.

Thus, he can be of either great assistance or hindrance, depending on his humour. If you want the right time and the right caddie on the important days, you keep well in with Bob. For two things are well-known. Firstly, the relationship between caddie and player can be critical to the final score and, dare I say it, is closer than the bonds of marriage, even if only for the duration of 18 holes of golf. Secondly, there are morning players and there are afternoon players, and for either caste to get the wrong time would be fatal to their ambitions in an important competition such as the Captain's or President's Prizes. (Something to do with their metabolism, I think.) Considering that such a win could be a man's passport through the Gates of Heaven past St. Peter (a wily old nine-handicapper in his day), one can appreciate the need to get these factors right from the outset.

The importance of betting, or "having an interest," is central to many people's enjoyment of the game, and Bob's willingness to undertake this onerous task made him a god to many and a devil to a sizeable minority.

Among his other talents is a way with words that can, at times, be astounding, but whether he means to be or not is open to question. I recall on one occasion a lovely young but innocent local girl, who was helping out in the greenfee office for the summer, asking me for some assistance in securing a piece of loose carpet near her chair which was causing her to trip every time she went in and out.

She did not know that I'm the last person in the world to ask for advice of that nature, as my good (and saintly) wife will testify, and, indeed, frequently does, whether she is asked to or not, but I do happen to know where a solution to most problems of this nature can be found. I directed her to Bob's office, for I knew he maintained a stock of do-it-yourself gadgetry there that would do a hardware shop proud.

The lovely lass flounced across the first tee and, in the clear hearing of all the assembled caddies, golfers, and American visitors, asked Bob in her best West Clare accent, "I need something to stick a piece of carpet in the office, Mr. Dickins. Would you have any Mastik?"

Bob savoured the moment like a true master and then, when he was sure he had the attention of the entire company, replied, "Ah, shure, darling, I haven't masticated for years. Try one of the young lads."

She turned a bright red and beat a hasty retreat to the ladies' room, from which she refused to emerge until closing time. True gentleman that he was, though, Bob discreetly arranged for the offending piece of carpet to be firmly nailed in place and the young lady tripped up no more, literally or figuratively.

On another famous occasion, when he deigned to caddie himself for an elderly American visitor who was reputedly filthy rich, he was asked on the fifteenth fairway, after putting up with 14 holes of agonised duffing by his privileged client, "Would a 5-iron get me up to the green, caddie?"

"Eventually, sur," was the laconic reply.

Have you ever been to one of those famous restaurants patronised by the theatrical world? You know, with autographed photographs of all the rich and famous diners adorning the wall. Bob's office was like that. He had a very expensive camera, of undisclosed origin, permanently loaded with the best film O'Riordan's chemist shop in Ennistymon could supply, and, whenever a golfer of note came by, he would find himself being photographed with a beaming Bob, who occasionally allowed one of his lesser bag-carrying minions to lurk in the background.

Apart from the prestige this collection of photographs undoubtedly conferred on Bob, this procedure was also found to have a very beneficial effect on the size of the tip that was forthcoming at the end of the round. When the bold Bob, however, decided to increase his gross margin even further by omitting to use any film in the camera, thus eliminating the principal cost factor, I felt constrained to point out to him the inequity of the situation and the danger it posed to his position should it ever emerge in public, especially in the *Clare Champion* newspaper, with whose editor the Captain happened to be particularly friendly. Bob saw the light immediately, fine upstanding Christian that he is, and the subject never had to be raised again. Ever since then, oddly enough, I've never been asked for the full price of any purchase I've made in O'Riordan's chemist shop!

♣ Opposition ♣

———

"Well, Doc, what do you think of the news?" asked Bob Dickins, savouring the moment. The good doctor was fiddling with his bag while waiting for his three playing buddies to arrive on the tee. He looked up at Bob and immediately smelled a rat.

"What news?"

"You mean you haven't heard?" Bob prided himself in knowing most of what went on in Lahinch and the surrounding countryside before anyone else, and occasionally, before it happened. He got particular pleasure in bringing such news to those whom it most directly concerned.

"Haven't heard what?" said the doctor, unwilling to concede anything. Bob lit a leisurely filter-tipped cigarillo and let him stew for a moment longer.

"About the new doctor coming to the village."

"Bob, have you some sort of bet on with those bandits that I'm playing with today, saying a thing like that to upset me?"

"I swear by my father's putter that I have no interest in your game today. I was merely making conversation to pass the time."

Bob's father's putter was his most treasured possession so Doctor Joe knew he was not joking.

"Tell me what you know," he said urgently and moved closer to Bob's sliding window, conveniently situated beside the tee.

"Here come your buddies," said Bob, spying the trio coming up the path toward the tee. "Meet me in the snug of the Golfer's Rest after your game. I'll be off duty by then."

And he slid over the glass panel, cutting off any further conversation with Doctor Joe until he stumped up for a large Irish whiskey in the snug of that well-known hostelry, halfway up the main street of Lahinch.

The worry about the new development had not done the Doctor's game any good. He could not concentrate on the job in hand and his side lost not only the match but the "Lloyd" and the "Bye" as well. A tidy sum changed hands in the locker room afterward. He did not even get to drink some of it in revenge, as he had to dash off to the Golfer's Rest to spend even more money on drink for Bob, for he knew that good information did not come cheap.

"This had better be good, Bob Dickins, or your father's putter is for the slag heap," Doctor Joe growled as he set down the tray of drinks on the table.

"Doctor, Doctor, calm yourself," said Bob, enjoying himself. "Have I ever led you astray?"

Doctor Joe considered the ambiguous question for a moment and realised that whatever answer he made would show him up in a bad light, so he let it pass. He sipped his whiskey and said, "Tell me about this new arrival."

This was not a trivial matter for the doctor. For nine months of the year Lahinch was a very small place indeed and, whilst he had no ambitions for great wealth, he currently enjoyed a millionaire's lifestyle on a fairly moderate income and a cut in that income could have serious repercussions.

"New doctor has bought McDonagh's old place at the top of the village. Moving into residence next week."

Doctor Joe considered the news carefully. This was not good. Moving into residence meant that the new doctor would be there permanently, not just a few days a week or during the peak season. Serious opposition, indeed. Doctor Joe foresaw hard times coming. Less golf, more work, longer hours, fewer patients, less money. He knocked back the remainder of his drink and stood up to go.

"Thanks, Bob."

But Bob hadn't finished with him yet.

"You haven't heard the best bit yet."

The good doctor sat down slowly. Surely it couldn't get any worse!

"It's a lady doctor. Angela McNamara. Twenty-seven years old, unmarried."

The name was vaguely familiar to Doctor Joe. A lady doctor. This was a disaster. A lot of women nowadays preferred lady doctors and, if they started going to her, the kids would soon follow and he'd be left with all the old men in the parish. He left the pub silently, a troubled man.

His analysis was spot on. His income dropped. The women turned to her in droves. He had to survive on hernias and in-grown toenails. His game went to pot.

He met her socially several times and got on famously with her and all the time she seemed vaguely familiar. She didn't play golf, which was one blessing at least, as this left him with some few patients. She was very pleasant and he could find no fault with her as a person, but he was feeling the pinch in his practice. At a drinks party before Christmas he got talking to her in a group, when she complained about how busy she was and about how little time she had to herself. He thought in amazement, *That never happened to me, especially in the winter.* He sympathised with her and claimed that he was having similar trouble. This was only a white lie, as he was indeed putting more effort into his practice but the results were not at all satisfactory. He spent a lot of time waiting for patients, being available and doing night calls, with the result that his golf had suffered. He could see himself going into double figures in handicap soon, if this kept up.

Then the germ of an idea started to develop in the back of his mind. He made a conscious effort to spend more time with Dr. Angela McNamara. Whenever they met socially he was very solicitous. He "accidentally" met her on some of the walks she took regularly around the hills and beaches of Lahinch and even took her to a movie and dinner in Limerick a few times.

When she returned the favour by inviting him to dinner in her home, he judged it the time right to make his move.

"Angela, that was an extraordinarily good pork steak. The stuffing was divine. How can you possibly combine such good cooking with a busy practice? Most of my food comes out of cans and the deep freeze."

"My mother gave me a good grounding before she let me loose on the world," she replied, smiling.

"Well, you can tell her from me that she did a fine job. Tell me now, you wouldn't be offended if I made a little suggestion to you, would you?"

"A suggestion, indeed! What's a girl to make of this, all of a sudden?"

"Oh, it's nothing, really. It's just something that's been going around in my head for a while. I was wondering how you would feel about amalgamating our practices. I could see benefits for both of us."

He stared intently into his drink as she considered the proposition. Then she leaned toward him and looked deep into his eyes.

"Does this mean that we'll be sleeping together?"

It was as well that Dr. Joe had built up a strong constitution over the years with all the golf he had played. He was poleaxed. She had misunderstood him totally. He had intended a simple business transaction. What was he to say? He realised that the wrong reaction could ruin everything. He tried to breathe deeply and then, to gain more thinking time, he took a large mouthful of brandy. This was a mistake. He was not used to it and he nearly choked on it. Fortunately, there was a doctor in the house and she had him back to normal in no time.

"Well," she asked him, smiling, "what should I make of that reaction?"

"I, uh, well, what I meant was, ahem..."

She put a finger to his lips, a sensation he found quite pleasant, and stopped him speaking.

"Do you recall a girl you took to the Med Ball in your final year at UCC?"

So that's where he had met her before!

"That girl was me. I was in Second Med at the time and I developed the most awful crush on my date at that Ball. For some extraordinary reason which I cannot explain, that crush has remained with me ever since. When I accidentally learned that you were in practice in Lahinch, I decided to come here and see if it was still alive."

She leaned closer and kissed him softly on the lips.

"It is. Now, if we get into bed together, do we get into bed together, if you see what I mean?" she asked him again. He saw exactly what she meant, and finally managed to blurt out.

"But Angela, what would Monsignor O'Flaherty say?"

She looked deep into his eyes, smiled sweetly and said, "I now pronounce you man and wife!"

❧ THE DAME FROM DOORADOYLE ❧

"SOMETHING WILL HAVE to be done!" said the Lady Captain. "We cannot go on like this. We are the premier club in the county and it's just not good enough that we haven't reached a Munster Final with any team for the last three years."

"What about the Minors two years ago?" Miss Duckett intervened.

"Dorothea, I meant teams of some significance," the Lady Captain glared, daring the outspoken one to contradict her. Dorothea decided that life was too short. The Lady Captain continued.

"We must put in place a strategy to improve our teams."

"Do you mean to bring in some 'ringers' from other clubs and beat the pants off everyone?" chimed in the lovely but light-headed Lily Lenihan brightly.

"I most certainly do not," hissed the Lady Captain icily, silencing the unfortunate Lily for the rest of the meeting. "I mean that we should put a coaching scheme in place, firstly, to encourage some new young players to join the Club, and, secondly, to improve the skills of our existing players."

"Here, here," said the Honorary Competition Secretary, Zena Raferty, who had been primed to support the Lady Captain on this matter well before the meeting took place.

"I know someone who only took up the game in the past year or so but who should be very good in time," Mary O'Regan said. "She played hockey for Ireland." The newest Member of the Ladies' Committee gazed expectantly toward the head of the table.

"Indeed," beamed the Lady Captain. "Has she joined a club yet?"

"No, she plays at one of those pay-as-you-play courses near Limerick."

"Hmmm, why don't you invite her here for a game next week. Zena and I will play a round with you to get some idea of her potential. We can discuss it further at the next meeting in a month's time. Is that okay with everyone? Right, let's move along. We've lots to get through yet."

And so it came to pass that Dily Donworth arrived in Lahinch. When she drove the par-4 thirteenth in the course of her "trial" round with the Lady Captain and the Honorary Competition Secretary, she could have had Honorary Life Membership on the spot as far as Zena was concerned. But the Lady Captain was a cannier old bird altogether. Afterward in the Locker Room, Zena and Mary were taken aside by the Lady Captain and told that, on pain of the most excruciating social ostracisation, they were not to mention to anyone what they had witnessed that day. The pair were so intimidated that neither of them ever claimed any credit for having introduced Dily to the club.

An emergency Ladies' Committee meeting was called for the next week to discuss the pressing matter of the new colour scheme for the ladies' loos and, almost as an afterthought, a recommendation was nodded through for the Men's Committee that Ms. Dily Donworth from Dooradoyle would be the Lady Captain's nomination for membership that year.

Dily was quickly put under the wing of Old Walter Partridge, one of the best teachers of the game in the Province, so that she would not develop any bad habits during her introduction to the game. One should mention here, perhaps, that the appellation "Old" Walter Partridge was in no way a reflection on the Professional's age or ability, but merely a convenient way to differentiate between him and "Young" Walter Partridge, who was beginning to make his presence felt in Junior golfing circles, much to the satisfaction of Mum and Pop.

Walter soon got the basics right and broke some potentially disastrous little habits that had crept in, even at that early stage. He had great difficulty, however, in breaking the ingrained hockey habit of a short backswing. If the truth be known, this did not make a great deal of difference to Dily, whom the Good Lord had endowed with ample musculature on a rather large frame, and who could, consequently, generate incredible clubhead speed with a relatively short arc to her swing. It also had the considerable benefit of keeping the ball very straight, as there was so little to go wrong.

Between Walter, Zena, and the benevolent Lady Captain, the new member made rapid progress and played several matches that year as she proceeded down the handicap range and became eligible for ever more "significant" teams. The following year, she became the leading light on the Ladies' Junior Cup Team and was largely responsible for getting them to not only the Munster Final, but also to the National Final itself. For Dily had the useful knack of intimidating her opponents into thinking that she was unbeatable and invariably finished her own match in time to go and lend both moral and vocal support to her teammates. Dily's vocal support was quite considerable, after years of issuing orders on the hockey field. This is not to suggest that she intimidated her teammates' opponents, too, but one or two of them were observed to become decidedly unnerved shortly after her arrival.

The National Finals were held that year at Ballybunion, a world-famous seaside links course, like Lahinch. It was just down the coast and across the Tarbert Car Ferry over the River Shannon in County Kerry. They scraped through the semis by the odd match. In the afternoon Finals, they were due to meet a well-known club from Leinster which had a reputation for "specialising" in Ladies' Junior Cup teams. But this club had not reckoned on Dily Donworth, the Dame from Dooradoyle.

She blitzed their number one player by seven and six (or a "dog license," as it's known amongst old timers), and sent the poor girl from the course in tears. Her roars of support for each of the other girls on the Lahinch team could be heard on the New Course next door, and several spectators suspected that the vibrations from her vocal chords added yards to drives and vital inches to putts. Even the former Lady Captain, who was now the Ladies' Junior Cup Team Manager, was moved to say,

very quietly, "Now, now, Dily, a little decorum, if you please."
But to no avail!

They brought the Ladies' Junior Cup home to Lahinch in
triumph and Dily went on to play Senior Cup the next year and,
inevitably, International for Ireland. She had umpteen boy-
friends but none of them could cope with her exuberance. She
never married. But she was something else, was Dily Donworth,
the Dame from Dooradoyle.

ᑐ᙭ THE O.G.S. ᙭ᑐ

THE OLDEST GOLFING SOCIETY is one of the most prestigious in the west of Ireland, if not the whole country. It is composed of the cream of Limerick gentry, the upper echelons of County Clare Movers and Shakers, and a sprinkling of the Upwardly Mobile. Each and every one is a Real Golfer.

Since its inception way back in the mists of time, there has been a strict limit of 60 members in the OGS, all men, which cannot be exceeded under any circumstances. It has, on occasion, not been fully taken up, due to a dearth of candidates considered suitable. But never exceeded.

The procedure is for any vacancies to be notified to current members at the beginning of each year and this information is then disseminated amongst the golfing brethren by word of mouth. Nothing as uncouth as advertising is involved.

Applicants have to give a brief resumé of their golfing and working careers to date, and the list is then whittled down to six. These lucky ones are invited to play a round on a particular day with the President, Captain, and Honorary Secretary of the OGS in three three-balls, before a final selection is made by these officers of the Society. Reasons for acceptance or rejection are never given, but each and every member of the OGS has to be a Real Golfer.

One may well speculate on what constitutes a Real Golfer, as opposed to the unreal variety. He is a difficult bird to pin down and is, perhaps, better identified by what he *does* rather than by what he *is*. He never misses an opportunity for a game of golf, births, deaths, and marriages excepted. Weather is no consideration but, oddly enough, the quality and design of a course are of paramount importance. Many a Real Golfer has sat on the beach or watched a football match (or even, God between us and all harm, cut the grass!) on a sunny day with a third-rate course convenient to him. But the same gent would travel miles out of his way to get a game on a first-class course in the most appalling conditions and in the face of the most rabid domestic dissension.

Money is not really a consideration either, once a certain minimum standard of dress can be maintained. Membership of a good club would be important, but dedicated golfers from lesser clubs have been accepted. Not many OGS play in Mixed Foursomes, but, in recent years, with all this women's liberation stuff, a blind eye has had to be turned on this particular transgression, as a gesture toward political correctness.

They only have six outings in a year and, by tradition, the first and last outings are held in Lahinch and one outing is held far afield, sometimes even in another country. They all sit down together for a special meal afterward, every man jack of them in a tuxedo! The OGS are not accompanied by their womenfolk.

I had the awful experience of mistakenly giving one of their traditional dates to another society in my first year, and it nearly blighted my career. Fortunately, the Honorary Secretary of the society concerned was an understanding chap and susceptible to bribes, so, in return for several free four-balls and the pick of dates for the following year, he let me off the hook. Upsetting the OGS was not an option.

One final peculiarity of this fine body of gentlemen was that they insisted that their members carry their own golf bags. No carts or caddies were allowed during their outings. This custom probably harked back to the good old days when men were men and there were no carts anyway. In more modern times it had the beneficial effect of ensuring a constant flow of retirees from the older members who could no longer keep up—rather like those Eskimo tribes that dump their elderly when they can no longer contribute to the economic well-being of the group. Slow play was anathema to the OGS, so when a player started hitting three and a half hours for a round of golf in normal conditions in a three-ball, the writing was on the wall for him. Speed up or ship out!

One year there was only a single vacancy, not an unusual situation in such a prestigious society. The usual six suspects were lined up for the "interview on the links." One unfortunate candidate had a wedding to go to on the day appointed and was disqualified upon his failure to turn up. He didn't talk to his wife for a month and never made it into the OGS thereafter.

Another poor sod crashed his car on the way to the course and, although not seriously injured, was carted off, protesting loudly, to the General Hospital in Ennis and was, consequently, out of the race, too. He was only dissuaded from suing the ambulance service and the Western Health Board for his disqualification on the promise that he would be guaranteed a place in the final six at the next available opportunity. His determination finally saw him through and he was elected the following year. He remained a member until he passed away during a thunderstorm at an outing in Waterville, County Kerry, many years later.

One of the remaining candidates was foolish enough to admit that he was slightly hung over from a party the night before and forfeited his chance on the spot. The OGS take their drinking seriously, but after golf, never before.

That left three little piggies, if you will excuse the expression. The odd number created a small problem for the officers but the matter was quickly resolved when a former President and Captain of the august society happened along and were invited to make two four-balls. In that way, two candidates played with two current officers and one played with one current officer and two former officers. Jim Nagle was considered unlucky to be in the latter four-ball, as he had the stress of coping with three prominent OGS and, in addition, was asked to play with the current Captain. Jim was a newly appointed, full-time, temporary teacher in the Ennistymon Secondary School and, if the truth be known, found golf a bit of a strain on his meagre finances. Indeed, his old banger of a car, long overdue for service, had only barely gotten him there on time that day.

The remaining two were Jack McGlynn, a supermarket owner from up the county, and Ger O'Driscoll, a prominent Limerick builder. This group set off first and the candidates behaved themselves impeccably, adding just the right touch of jocularity to the serious four-ball on hand and finishing all flat into the bargain.

Jim Nagle started badly, due to a severe case of nervous tension, and his situation was not helped by the fact that his partner, the Captain, was having a seriously off day. The stake of 20 pounds was a bit out of his depth, too, and a loss that afternoon, bearing in mind the probability of several drinks in the bar afterward, and the need to get the car exhaust fixed before he was arrested for noise pollution, meant that for the rest of the month he would be painfully impecunious.

He tried hard to pull himself together and after nine holes he had managed to limit the damage to three down. They were in serious trouble. Considering that their opponents were dyed-in-the-wool OGS of many years standing, he had an uphill battle on his hands.

With the aid of a few spectacular putts and dynamite chipping, but still with no help from his partner, the Captain, Jim got the match to all flat after 17 holes. With his tail up, Jim blasted two woods to within six feet of the last green. His partner was on the road, looking for his pulled second shot, and the opposition was on in three but in no danger of getting a birdie. The two former officers walked around the back of the green while Jim lined himself up for his shot. As he addressed the ball, it moved about an inch. It meant a one-shot penalty because he would be deemed to have caused the movement! His mind was in turmoil. Should he keep silent about the penalty shot or should he tell? This quandary so flummoxed him that he lost his concentration, hit a poor chip and failed to sink the putt.

His opponents both putted out for fives to half the hole and the match, as they thought. The Captain, who had rejoined the party after his sojourn on the roadway, was delighted.

"Well done, Jim! That's one of the best comebacks I've ever seen and you managed it with no help from me at all." Jim hesitated and muttered something under his breath.

"What's that, lad?"

"I'm afraid I've bad news for you, Mr. Captain. My ball moved just as I addressed it and I incurred a one-stroke penalty. I had a six, so we actually lost the match."

The Captain was not amused.

As he was going home in his noisy old banger after a few very uncomfortable drinks in the bar upstairs, Jim was not a happy man. Three days later a small package arrived in the post. It contained a black bow tie and a short note from the Captain of the OGS:

"The OGS members are sticklers for the Rules. Welcome to the Society."

᪥ OLD EAGLE EYE ᪥

———

THE FUNERAL WAS a grand affair. Nearly the whole village of Lahinch was there, with many a person travelling from Liscannor, Lisdoonvarna, Miltown Malbay, and beyond, Miss Robson was so well thought of. The fine drapery shop on Main Street was closed for the day, of course, but at 9:00 o'clock the next morning it was open again. Business was business, after all.

Everyone assumed that her cousin, Ann O'Shea, a popular young lady member of Lahinch Golf Club, who had effectively been running the shop for the past five years, would inherit it as a going concern. Everyone, that is, except Harold Robson, Miss Robson's long-lost nephew, who turned up on the doorstep exactly one week after the poor old woman had been laid to rest. The man had impeccable timing.

As the bold Harold had not been seen nor heard of in Lahinch since his teens and was now in his late thirties, he had been forgotten and, it was assumed, was no longer of this earth, in common with the rest of his clan, which seemed to have a predilection for early mortality. He and cousin Ann were the only two left breathing God's good air, which made the fact that the late Miss Robson had not made a will all the more interesting. For Harold, that is, not for Ann. He claimed everything.

The village was stunned and then horrified, when it was discovered that he planned to sell the prime property on Main Street and depart with what everybody now regarded as his ill-gotten gains, however legitimately he had come into them. Despite the great sympathy that welled up for Ann, there was, apparently, nothing that anybody could do about it, so she had to continue to run the shop from week to week, while Mr. Harold besported himself about the area, enjoying the fruits of her labours, waiting for the estate to be settled. The only time he called into the shop was to take some "drawings" from the petty cash, which now had to be replenished several times each week, instead of once a month as heretofore.

Some time after his arrival in Lahinch, Harold Robson was invited by one of the members to play golf at the links. Not having any equipment with him, he went into the Pro Shop at the Club to hire the necessary gear from Walter Partridge, the professional of some 20 years standing in the Club.

"Have you any decent clubs for hire, my good man?" enquired Harold imperiously.

"All my hire equipment is decent, young man," replied Walter, with just a touch of frost in his tone. "Did you have anything in particular in mind?"

Realising that Walter was no pushover, Harold modified his attitude and asked to see what was available. He made his selection and took a cart as well.

Satisfied that he had Harold where he wanted him, Walter went on the offensive with a few questions.

"Planning to stay long? Perhaps I could interest you in a new set of clubs, and perhaps one of these Yonex drivers that are all the rage now? Gives an extra 30 yards on your drive, I'm told."

"Possibly. I'll have to see how things go before I decide."

"Didn't I give you lessons one summer long ago when you were visiting your aunt, God rest her?"

"Indeed, indeed," blustered Harold, beating a hasty retreat. "I'll take a dozen of these balls as well."

"Thank you, sir," said Walter, delighted with the extra sale. But he looked thoughtfully after the man as he left his shop.

Harold went into the locker room to change and, when he emerged a few minutes later, Walter made a point of watching him and his partner on the first tee, which was in plain sight of the Pro Shop. They spent a few minutes fussing about with their equipment, getting balls out, looking for tees, ball markers, pitch mark repairers, and the like, before taking a few practice swings to warm up.

Watching the two men on the tee swinging the clubs, Walter said to himself, "Well now, would you look at that?"

He took the key out of the till, grabbed his jacket and a club out of his own bag, and headed off, locking the door carefully behind him. Casually, using the club as a walking stick, he sauntered up the first fairway after the two golfers, keeping a sharp eye on Harold, particularly when it was his turn to play. He watched them play off the second tee before following them back down the hill to the clubhouse. However, instead of returning to the Pro Shop, he got into his car and drove out of the Club with a pensive frown on his face and made his way to the local Garda Station, where he called in and asked for Sergeant Twomey. They chatted for a while and then Walter returned to the Pro Shop. Three hours later the Sergeant left the Garda Station and headed for the Golf Club, just in time to see Harold Robson and his companion leave the eighteenth green at the end of their round. He went into the bar and waited for Harold to appear.

"Mr. Robson, a private word, if you please."

Harold Robson looked startled for a moment and then, smiling nonchalantly, walked over to the corner where the Sergeant, in full uniform, was waiting. They chatted quietly for about 10 minutes and then the Sergeant thanked him politely for his time and left. In the dark of that night, Harold Robson departed from Lahinch and was never heard of again.

The following week a handful of people were gathered in the office of Jarlath J. McKeown, Solicitor.

"Well, my dear, I'm glad to say that I have some excellent news for you," J.J. McKeown beamed across at Ann O'Shea. "Thanks to some excellent detective work by the good Sergeant and Mr. Partridge, your inheritance is safe, and the so-called 'Harold Robson' will not be bothering you again."

Ann's mouth dropped open. She looked on, speechless, as the Sergeant took up the story.

"Yes, indeed, Ann, it seems that our friend 'Harold' was an impostor. He knew the real Harold in Australia before he died, heard the family history from him over a period of time and, by an extraordinary series of coincidences, he ended up in Ireland just as Miss Robson's death was announced in the papers. He had intended sponging off the family for a while on the strength of having known the real Harold before he died, but realised that he could make a killing when he found that you were the only known heir and Harold's death was still unreported. If it weren't for our eagle-eyed old Pro here, he might well have gotten away with it."

"Why, Mr. Partridge, however did you know that it was not the real Harold?" Ann managed to ask.

"Well, Ann," began Walter, enjoying his moment in the limelight, "I first realised that something was wrong when I saw him swinging his club on the first tee the other day while warming up before a game. A golf swing is a very personal thing, almost like handwriting or a fingerprint. After all my long years in the teaching business, I can identify most people that I have taught by their swing. And an awful lot that I have not taught as well, just by keen observation. It is, theoretically, possible to change a swing, as it might be to change handwriting, if you assiduously worked at it over a period of time. But for most people, especially amateur golfers, you are stuck with what the Good Lord gave you from the minute you take up this cursed game. The young Harold came to me for lessons many years ago while in Lahinch visiting his aunt one summer, and I rarely forget a swing. It seemed to me that it was not the same swing that I remembered, so I had a few words with the Sergeant here, who made a few enquiries and then had a little chat with 'Harold'."

"Yes," said the Sergeant laughing, "I got nothing conclusive out of that conversation but it obviously spooked yer man and he took off. Naturally, I followed up with my colleagues Down Under after that and it was established that the real Harold had died during a hike in the outback with some companions, one of whom was our impostor. I'm glad to say that he has fled the jurisdiction, so this matter can be quietly laid to rest here and now. You can get what is rightly yours and the nosey parkers of the town need be none the wiser."

And true to his word, they weren't.

❧ The President's Wife's Niece ❧

———

"I'M SURE YOUR wife's niece is a lovely girl, Mr. President, but that is not the way I was given to understand that the staff were to be appointed around here. The selection and appointment of staff was to be solely at the discretion of the Secretary/Manager. No undue influence was to be brought to bear."

"All I'm asking, Mr. Manager, is that you give her an interview when the time comes for taking on additional staff. I would, of course, be ever so grateful if she happened to be selected."

I could see that the man was determined, so I muttered something noncommittal and changed the subject.

Some time later I had the opportunity to discuss the matter confidentially with Dr. Joe Moore, and his advice was not to cross the influential president. The man's tentacles spread far and wide, and the repercussions, if he was offended, would be swift and silent, with the distinct possibility of being fatal as well. Considering the pressure the man must be under from his wife, it was clear that he would suffer a severe loss of face in that quarter if he failed to secure his desired objective, thus making him even more dangerous and vindictive. On the other hand, it could be very useful to have such a person in your corner, should any favours be needed in the future. With these dire warnings and predictions ringing in my ears, I felt that I had no real alternative. When the time came, Miss Susan Monaghan got the job.

She was pretty enough, in a West of Ireland sort of way, all red hair and freckles, but she was completely inexperienced and more than a little awkward. I made a silent promise to myself that if I could get rid of her without doing myself damage, I would, at the earliest opportunity.

On her first day in the greenfee office she made such a mess of the cash that it was impossible to match up the tickets issued with the money taken. This was the first time that such a thing had happened since I had taken over at the Club as Secretary/ Manager. It was clear that it was a genuine mistake and that there was nothing sinister in it, so I let it pass, blaming myself to some extent for leaving her unsupervised for too long, as two of the other girls were out with the flu at the time. The trembling lips and glistening eyes did not help the situation, either. I was not amused.

One of the duties of most new arrivals in an office is to look after the "elevenses" in the morning, and our little kingdom was no exception. The next day, expecting the same standard of service as usual, I took a large gulp from my special half-pint mug of coffee which she had brought in, 10 minutes late, and nearly burned the mouth off myself. She had misjudged the amount of milk necessary to render the scalding brew palatable in a mug of those proportions, being used to more dainty crockery at her aunt's house, no doubt. I insisted on separate milk and coffee from then on and did the honours myself.

Shortly after her arrival, our filing system began to break down. Maybe "break down" is too strong a description, but items disappeared into it never to be seen again, unless by accident. When the Captain complained that some of his correspondence appeared to be going astray, I hit the panic button, for it is well known in golf club management circles that unhappy Captains make for unhappy Managers. When Miss Monaghan was moved to other duties, the system mysteriously began to function properly again.

I suppose I should not have allowed her anywhere near the computer, with a track record like that, but we were under pressure and everyone had to pull their weight. Backing up the files at the end of the day is a fairly simple, straightforward job, with very little to go wrong. Unless, that is, you happen to instruct the machine to copy the data from the removable floppy disc onto the fixed hard disc, instead of the other way round, thus wiping out all the work recorded on the hard disc in the time since the last backup. It took several hours of frantic, and expensive, overtime to rectify the situation.

I'm not usually a difficult person to work for, preferring encouragement to admonition, but I really let fly at this young lady after that incident. I confess that I may have overdone it a bit, so much so that she broke down in floods of tears in my office and I was forced to comfort the poor girl by resting her head on my shoulder and patting her back. It took her some time to compose herself, and all the while I was feeling guiltier by the minute.

Eventually she calmed down enough for me to send her back to work, but for the rest of the day I couldn't get rid of the memory of how pleasant it had been holding her.

I tried to put such thoughts out of my mind and got on with my work. A few days later I happened to be covering the greenfee office at lunchtime while the girls were out, when I was accosted by two irate foreigners, one of whom spoke only French and the other only German, and it was obvious that they were not on the friendliest of terms. My ignorance of both languages did not help the situation one little bit, and things were getting quite out of hand when Miss Monaghan appeared from the back office.

"Can I help?" she asked.

I gave her a pitying look and said, "I doubt it."

She ignored my ungallant remark and proceeded to tackle the babbling Europeans, using fluent French and German in turn to sort out their problem.

Needless to say, I was gobsmacked. Digging deep into my paltry reserves of humility, I apologised for my crassness and then enquired what the problem had been with the foreigners.

"It seems that they are both big travel agents in their own countries and both had groups ready to play off the first tee. They were quarrelling about who should go first, as they had all arrived together. I established that they were all staying for two days, so I sent one lot off to the Castle Course and booked them in for 10 o'clock on the Old Course tomorrow morning, and vice versa with the other group."

"Two travel agents, you say! That could have been serious. I'm most obliged to you, Miss Monaghan. You handled the situation very well. I'll have to owe you one for that."

"You can owe me two," she retorted cheekily.

"How do you mean?"

"You can stop calling me Miss Monaghan like some middle-aged spinster. My name is Susan. And there is a new James Bond movie on in Limerick this week that I'd love to see."

What could I do? I was cornered, with no way out. I decided there and then that she definitely had to go, no matter what.

I agreed, somewhat ungraciously, to take her to the new Bond movie. But I did get rid of her eventually, in a manner of speaking. Two years later I married her (or was it she who married me?), much to the horror of the president's wife, who had great plans of her own for this young lady. So she doesn't take orders from me at the Golf Club any more, but she does allow me to give the odd instruction at home, from time to time, provided, of course, that it does not conflict with what she has already decided herself.

❧ The Grapes of Wrath ❧

———

THE NEW MEMBER was a Belgian, retired from the European Headquarters in Brussels. He was recently elected a member and was paying me his entrance fee plus the annual subscription to complete the membership formalities.

"I hope you enjoy your retirement, Richard," I said as I handed him the bag tag and receipt that pronounced him a member of Lahinch Golf Club, "and that your handicap soon comes down to single figures."

"Zhank you so much," he replied, with only a hint of an accent. "I am looking forward to playing zis fine course again. I have enjoyed it many times during my vacances over the years. Is there likely to be anybody around at zis time of the day to play with?"

"Things are a bit quiet just now," I said, "but let's have a look outside and see if there is anyone looking to be 'fixed-up'." I was glad of the excuse to get up off my behind and stretch my legs in the fresh air.

"'Fixed-up'," he echoed, smiling. "What a curious expression. I understand exactly what you mean, but I must tell you that in Europe it means something entirely different, involving ladies of the night. Eh ha, comprenez vous?" He laughed.

"Indeed, indeed," I said, laughing as well. "That meaning has some currency here, too, but in a strictly amateur sense." We trooped down the stairs together, men of the world sharing a little risqué joke.

There was nobody on the seat in front of the downstairs office, a favourite spot for players waiting for a game. Nor on the practice green or in the car park.

"Let's try the Pro Shop," I said, and we strolled over to Old Walter's hideaway.

"Walter, this is Richard Broussard, recently retired from Brussels and now a fully-fledged member of Lahinch Golf Club."

Walter is not one little bit slow when it comes to sniffing out a potentially lucrative transaction, and I could just see the ECUs clocking up inside his head. He welcomed M. Broussard profusely.

"And if there is anything I can do for you," Walter said, concluding his welcoming speech, "do not hesitate to ask."

Providing him with an opening, I said, "Well, Richard is looking for a game, if anyone turns up."

Walter hesitated for a moment, obviously caught between two minds. Just then, a voice from the back of the shop chimed in. Jammy Flaherty said in his most ingratiating manner, "I'd love to show our new member around the Old Course." He came forward with outstretched hand and I could smell trouble at once. "James Flaherty at your service. Fifteen handicap. And yourself?"

"Richard Broussard," our new member replied. "I am pleased to meet you. I play off 12 but I have not been very active recently, with all the moving of the house and so on." They shook hands. I could see that Jammy liked the sound of what he heard.

"Never mind that," he said. "You'll soon get back into the swing of things."

But not before the bold Jammy cleans him out first, I thought to myself. And sure enough the next words out of his mouth were "How much will we play for?"

I managed to catch Richard's eye and give a slight shake of my head to warn him off this well-known "shark," so he said, "I don't like to play for money so soon. How about a glass of wine on the loser when we finish?"

"A glass of wine?" laughed Jammy. "Sure, with the size of the glasses they use here you'd hardly wet the inside of your mouth. I'll tell you what. Make it a bottle and we'll have a good game. Winner chooses."

After only a momentary hesitation, Richard agreed, no doubt figuring that even if he lost he could drink half the wine anyway.

"A caddie, a caddie, my kingdom for a caddie," roared Jammy with great glee as he made his way out the door toward Bob Dickins's Caddiemaster's Office.

I shrugged my shoulders and smiled sympathetically at Richard.

"Relax and enjoy the scenery," I advised. "The worst that can happen is that you will have to buy the wine."

Richard laughed graciously. "Fear not," he said. "It will not be the first bottle of wine that I have had to buy in my time." He waved and followed Jammy out of the shop.

"What an introduction to Lahinch!" exclaimed Walter. "I wouldn't wish it on my worst enemy. I hope Jammy gets a dose of the word that rhymes with 'rockets.'"

This was the worst affliction that one could wish on a golfer, consisting of a tendency to hit the ball with the hosel of the club instead of the blade, thus causing the ball to fly off at almost right angles to the desired line of flight. One never used the actual word of "sockets" for fear of getting a dose merely by thinking about them. Coming from a gentleman like Walter, this imprecation indicated a very strong disapproval of Mr. Flaherty indeed. With that caustic curse ringing in my ears, I headed off to my office, making a mental note to be sure to come down and meet the gladiators as they came off the eighteenth green in about three and a half hours time.

Richard turned out to be a tougher nut to crack than Jammy had expected. Walter's curse apparently had some effect, too, because he had three of the vile "rockets" at vital stages in the match, so that when they came to the fifteenth hole, the last one going north, away from the clubhouse, he found himself one down with four to play. Not a disastrous situation, but just a wee bit uncomfortable.

They both got good drives away and Richard had to play first, as he was furthest away from the flagstick. He hit a superb three wood up the left side with a slight fade on it so that when it hit the ground it bounced right and headed straight for the flag.

"There was a touch of 'local knowledge' about that one," exclaimed Jammy grudgingly.

"I have played zis shot sometimes before on my holidays," explained Richard patiently, and for the first time in the round Jammy felt the icy grip of fear around his fluttering heart.

In stony silence, Jammy marched up to where his ball waited for further punishment. He turned to his young caddie and, for the first time in the round, asked for his advice on what club to play. The young lad had given up paying much attention to Jammy way back at the fourth hole when he realised that he was going to be a mere bag carrier for that day and his fledgling wisdom would not be required by the soaring eagle that Jammy imagined himself to be. Thus he was caught completely off guard by Jammy's question.

Trying desperately to get his wits together, he dropped the bag in an attempt to gain a little time for thought. Jammy was not amused.

"Come on, come on. What is it in there? It can only be one of three clubs."

Bugger! thought the young lad. *Which one of the three?*

Doing a quick calculation in his head, he figured it was either a three-, four- or five-iron. He decided to play safe.

"With your power, sur, a four-iron should do the job nicely."

Somewhat mollified by the calculated compliment, Jammy accepted the four-iron proffered by the now fully attentive caddie.

If the truth be known, it would not have mattered what club the youngster suggested, as there was no way that Jammy was going to get the ball anywhere near that green, such was the volcanic pressure building up inside his head. For he had just realised that if he lost this hole he would be two down with only three holes left to play and in dire straits indeed.

He duly lunged at the ball and took out a divot that started at least two inches behind the ball and travelled on for a further nine inches past the spot where it had lain. The ball did not get on the green.

"Ye blind little gurrier!" roared Jammy. "It was never a four-iron." He grabbed the bag from the young lad and shoved him away. "Be off with ye, you useless piece of garbage. I'll be telling Bob Dickins you're good for nothing. You'll get no caddie's fee out of me this day." And off he stalked. Richard was not amused, but years of diplomatic training prevented him from saying anything.

The match duly ended on the seventeenth. Richard holed out for a good bogey and won by two and one. Jammy had been unable to best him on either of the last two holes. The eighteenth was played out in deathly silence.

Walter and I met them coming off the green. It was obvious from their respective demeanours what the result was, but neither of us could resist putting the boot into Jammy.

"How did the game go, gentlemen?" I enquired.

"Yes, indeed, Jammy," chipped in Walter, as only he could. "Did you show our visitor a good time?"

The scowl on Jammy's face would have stopped a thundercloud from dropping its deluge on the dunes.

"Iwasbeatenbytwoandone," he mumbled.

"You won by two holes, Jammy?" asked Walter, the old devil, rubbing it in.

Jammy had had enough. He decided to face up to his tormentors. "I was beaten by two and one," he enunciated clearly and distinctly, "and now I am going to buy this gentleman a bottle of wine upstairs, if you don't mind."

"Upstairs?" asked Richard. "But who said anything about upstairs? I thought the winner got to choose?"

Catching his drift, Walter and I played along.

"That's right," Walter said. "I certainly recall Jammy saying those very words: 'the winner chooses.' Did you not also hear them, Mr. Secretary?"

"Why, Mr. Partridge, I believe I did. How could you have forgotten so soon, Mr. Flaherty? Whatever would your friends say?"

Jammy knew full well that it was not his few friends that I had in mind but rather his many enemies.

"Alright, alright," he conceded, "winner chooses." The plot had gone badly awry for Jammy.

"Would either of you gentlemen know of an establishment in the vicinity called P.J. Egan's?" Richard enquired politely. "I believe they keep a stock of good wines."

"Well, it so happens that I do," replied Walter. "I shall be only delighted to ride with you, and your good friend Mr. Jammy Flaherty, to those premises at your convenience. Mr. Secretary, will you join us?"

Wild pigs wouldn't keep me away.

Arriving at Egan's hostelry some 20 minutes later, Walter and I enjoyed the look of impending doom on Jammy's face as he entered the unfamiliar surroundings. Pints of black porter were more Jammy's style. He only agreed to the wine bet because he figured he was going to win and it would be free.

"Landlord," called Walter, really getting into the spirit of the occasion and milking it for all it was worth, clearly realising that there would be many a good pint sunk in the retelling of this tale, "a memorable bottle of wine for this gentleman. He has his retirement, his new membership and a great victory to celebrate."

Jammy's heart sunk. A wine good enough for a triple celebration. The pain of it.

Mr. Egan was no fool. He sensed at once that there was something afoot and played along beautifully.

"No ordinary wine would cover a situation like that. I shall have to check my cellar. Perhaps you gentlemen would care to refresh yourselves from this poor vintage that passes for a house wine, and with my compliments." He departed for the bowels of the building.

A solitary grandfather clock marked the passing of time with loud ticks. Everyone sipped the house wine, which would have, in fact, passed muster in some very good company indeed. In four minutes, Egan returned with a dust-covered bottle.

"A Chateau Ducru, Beaucaillou, '78. An excellent vintage and a snip at 40 pounds."

Jammy's heart sank to his boots. Richard gave a slight shake of his head and the astute Mr. Egan took the signal like a trooper.

"However, it is a trifle dry for some palates and the odd bottle has been found to be quite off."

"Oh, God no, that would never do," beamed Walter, twisting the knife in Jammy's fiscal gut even further. "This occasion is much too important to risk anything like that. Can you do no better?"

Mr. Egan's nostrils flared in mock horror at the implied insult and he marched off to his cellar again. This time the wait was seven minutes, during which time not a word was spoken.

"A Chateau Mouton Rothschild, Pauillac, '84," said the returned Mr. Egan, with a hint of exasperation, "and a personal favourite. Seventy-five pounds."

"Mmm, sounds good," said Walter, looking at me. I concurred.

"Indeed," said Richard. "Unfortunately, I received a retirement present of a bottle from my colleagues in Brussels only last week."

"Ah, too bad," smiled Mr. Egan, knowing he was onto a winner. "Let me see what else I can find."

By now Jammy was making protesting noises, but these stopped when three pairs of eyes turned on him in icy silence. It took Mr. Egan 10 full minutes to return with a dust-encrusted bottle whose label defied decoding but which the landlord assured us was a rare Chateau Lafite Rothschild, Pauillac, '82, probably the only one in the country, and he was prepared to part with it for a mere 150 pounds.

Jammy blanched.

Richard smiled and graciously accepted his trophy with great tenderness. As the dirty bottle nestled in the comfort of his arms, Jammy manfully managed to extract three 50-pound notes from his wallet and push them across the counter. He then made a very undignified exit.

The bottle was handed back across the counter to the landlord and, as he did the honours, Richard explained what had happened with the young caddie. We were all then invited to toast his retirement, his new membership, and his victory, with what proved to be truly the nectar of the gods from that filthy bottle. And it was made all the tastier by the fact that it was Jammy Flaherty's 50-pound notes that were in the till.

On our way back to Lahinch, along Millionaires Row, Richard suddenly pulled over to the side of the road. He rolled down the window and beckoned to a lad who was walking along inside the boundary wall of the Old Course.

"Young man," he called out, "weren't you the lad caddieing for my friend this afternoon?"

The lad approached the car and nodded his head. "Yes, sur, but I only got as far as the fifteenth hole."

"That's okay. My friend has a short fuse. He asked me to give you this 20-pound note for your trouble and to apologise for his behaviour. I don't think it will happen again."

The young lad's jaw dropped and he took the note from Richard. "Thank you, sur. I'm sure the four-iron was the right club, sur. But he needed to hit the *ball* first, not the *ground.*"

✃ On Yer Bike! ✃

———

Jody Millar was a tall, gangly lad, with a shock of curly black hair that was the envy of many a lass in Ennistymon. He was dead keen on golf and had a lovely short game. However, despite his height, which gave him a very long arc to his swing—which would normally allow a player to generate plenty of clubhead speed and thus distance—he was quite short off the tee. This was a great source of chagrin to Jody, not to mention embarrassment, because amongst male golfers of all ages big hitting is a very macho thing. He determined to rectify this deficiency in his game by exploiting his position as an only child and the apple of his mother's eye. His seventeenth birthday was coming soon and he decided to enlist her very willing support to rectify matters.

"Mam, can I have a new driver for my birthday?"

"Of course you can, Jody baby. Seventeen! My how time flies. I remember..."

"Thanks, Mam. You're a darling!" cut in Jody, who, much and all as he loved his dear old Mam, did not feel up to listening to another one of her rambling reminiscences. One of the few disadvantages of being an only child was having to listen to one's parents' constant babbling about subjects of no interest whatsoever to a young man about town. He made his escape up the stairs to his room, which he had recently managed, after much aggravation and prolonged negotiations, to have declared a DMZ (De-Mamized Zone). (The trials and tribulations of growing up!) There he plotted the second leg of his strategy: how to extract the necessary 300 pounds from his dad for the graphite-shafted driver of his dreams, one that was guaranteed to add 30 yards to his drives, if the advertising blurb was to be believed. This would be an altogether tougher proposition, for Dad was not the pushover his Mam was.

Sunday, after lunch, was the time selected to put his plan into action. His unsuspecting Dad would be relaxed and pleasantly fatigued after his usual morning round of golf in Lahinch, and would more than likely agree to anything, as long as he got a bit of peace and quiet to have a snooze. He had persuaded his Mam to do a beef Wellington as a special treat, and he figured that the combination of a full tummy and tired legs would do the trick. Mrs. Millar was famous for her sherry trifle in the region, so she added that to the menu, just in case.

As they were tucking in, Jody asked, in his most innocent tone, "Dad, can I have a new driver for my birthday next week?" If he had left it at that he might have gotten away with it. But, unwisely, he added, "All the other lads are longer off the tee than I am and I need something to catch up with them."

Alarm bells went off in Jackie Millar's head. Distance off the tee? That could only mean one thing: high prices. He knew this, because he himself was in the way of being seduced by the blandishments of the advertisements in the golf magazines that he bought, ostensibly for his son.

"What driver would that be, son?" he responded, equally innocently. It gave Jody a premonition that things were not going to go his way.

"That new Callaway, with the graphite shaft."

"Would that be the one that costs 300 pounds?"

"But Dad, I'll win that off the lads over the summer with the extra length I'll get off the tee."

"Win the money first, laddie, and then buy the driver yourself."

"Ahh, Daaad..."

"'Ah, Dad,' me eyeball! What do you think I'm made of? Do you think money grows on trees? You have two chances of getting that club, laddie: zero and none. Now let me be, so that I can enjoy my lunch and have a bit of a snooze."

Jody was desperate. He decided to try one more time and enlisted the aid of his mother.

"Mam, you said I could have that driver. What'll I do now? All the other lads will beat the socks off me during the summer."

Rose Millar hadn't said a word throughout this exchange. To tell the truth, she was somewhat taken aback at the price of the club in question. Why were men such suckers for golf equipment? Now, if that had been a nice two-piece suit from Todds in Limerick, she could understand. But a golf club? She then made a fatal error. She jumped in, feet first, on Jody's side.

"I really think, Jackie Millar, that you could stretch a point and get the boy that silly club. He'll be seventeen next week. Why, he's a young man. Our son should have the best equipment."

Oh, dear! That was the wrong thing to say. Hackles rose all the way down the spine of Jackie Millar, who had spent a goodly part of his working life providing amply for his only son, and he glared, uncharacteristically, at his wife.

"Roseanne Millar," he started (she knew she had overstepped the mark then, because her husband never called her Roseanne unless there was a serious spat coming), "in all the years that we've been married, have I ever stinted you or Jody for anything? He's had everything he ever set his heart on. He's spoilt rotten and it's mostly your fault. You just don't know how to say 'No'!"

Had this been a private conversation, Rose Millar might have let that remark pass, but, in front of her only, darling son, she took serious umbrage.

"I know how to say 'No' alright, as you'll find out in due course. How dare you speak to me like that!"

"See if I care!" he shot back, before his brain had time to analyze the consequences of what his mouth was saying. "He'll have that bicycle I'm going to buy for him in Ennis. I'm fed up running a taxi service for him from Ennistymon to Lahinch. He can cycle there himself from now on."

Rose Millar got up from the dining room table with all the dignity she could muster, and muttered through gritted teeth, "In that case, Jackie Millar, you won't mind sleeping in the spare room for a while. I feel one of my headaches coming on."

Jody was devastated. Not only was his new driver gone with the wind, but his Mam and Dad were at each other like a pair of racoons. Where had he gone wrong? And a bicycle! Holy God, he'd have to cycle all the way to Lahinch and back every time he wanted to play golf, or even do a little bit of practice. This was undoubtedly the worst day of his life.

It wasn't such a good day for Jackie Millar, either. An idyllic Sunday ruined! Just as the sherry trifle, which had had no small influence over his original decision to marry Roseanne Barry, as she was known in those days, was having the desired effect (i.e., oblivion without the hangover), the whole day was ruined by this turn of events. He was shattered but determined. It was time that Jody learned the facts of life. He couldn't have everything his heart desired, and the sooner he realised it, the better off he would be!

For six long weeks he suffered in solitary exile in the spare room. Rose wasn't budging an inch. Nor was he. The month of May would smile on the fair land of Lahinch before the ice melted. Jody cycled to the Club every time he wanted to play golf, or to practice. The first time, he was so tired when he arrived there that he bummed a lift straight home from a kindly neighbour, putting his bike in the boot of the car, and had to go for a lie-down to recover, once he got home. He learned a bit from that experience. The next time he went, he allowed more time, took it much easier and walked up the hills he encountered.

Thereafter, he went from strength to strength and, in no time at all, he was whizzing over and back to Lahinch from Ennistymon without a bother on him. He developed a fine pair of legs under him and, as a consequence, he slowly but surely, to his own delighted amazement, added yards to his drive as the weeks went by.

The Captain's Prize to juniors comes rather early in Lahinch, as the Competitions Committee likes to get as many Club competitions out of the way as possible, before the season gets under way. Thus, in early May, Jody took his place on the tee with his playing partners one Sunday morning at 11:16 and proceeded to blast his way round the Old Course in 68 shots net, the winning score by some margin.

That night, at tea in the Millar household, the young man proudly displayed his prize and the Captain's Trophy that the winner held for a year.

"Well done, son!" said Jackie, who had derived great enjoyment from buying his friends pints at the Club to celebrate his son's famous victory. "I never came within a smell of a prize like that when I was your age."

"Well, Dad, I hate to admit it, but that bike you got me for my birthday was a big help. I've a pair of thighs on me now like a lumberjack and I'm hitting the ball outside most of the other lads off the tee."

"Glad to be of assistance, son. But you had to do the work on the day. A magnificent achievement!"

"Yes, indeed, Jody baby. Very well done indeed! We're very proud of you."

"Ahhh, Mam, cut out that 'Jody baby' stuff, will ya? I'm not a baby any more!"

"Sure, I keep forgetting that you're nearly all grown up now, Jody. You'll have to forgive your old Mam."

"Not so old, there now," chimed in Jackie gallantly. "You could show some of those young ones a trick or two yet!" And he gave her a bit of a squeeze.

"Go on with you, Jackie Millar, you are awful!"

At this, Jody beat a hasty retreat to his room, for if there was one thing worse than his Mam and Dad rowing, it was the pair of them going all lovey-dovey.

"How about a kiss, Missus, to celebrate our son's famous victory?" Jackie was pushing his luck, but Rose duly obliged, for, to tell the truth, she was thoroughly fed up with living like a spinster.

Two minutes later, as she disengaged herself, slightly dizzy, from her husband's embrace, she said, "I have to spring clean that spare room tomorrow. You'd better move back in where you belong."

And thus it was that Jody Millar acquired his little sister, Joanna Roseanna Millar, who, in time, learned to wrap her Mam, her Dad, and her adoring big brother round her little finger with ease, and never, ever, failed to get what she wanted.

ᔓ Ma Clarke ᔓ

————

EVERY PARISH PRIEST in the country had a housekeeper, but only Monsignor Pius Ignatious O'Flaherty had Ma Clarke. When he first arrived in the little parish of Lahinch and Liscannor, he thought the woman was a paragon of virtue. He had never been so well looked after in his life. Even his late, sainted mother, God be good to her, didn't do as fine a job. The fact of the matter was that Ma Clarke (or Mrs. Martina Clarke, widow, to give her the full title) was a class above the lot of them when it came to looking after a man. Her late, beloved husband, Mossy, could have vouched for that. No man ever lived so high on the hog as he did for the 20 years or so that she ministered to him. His ample girth and increasingly ruddy complexion bore witness to that. Before the massive coronary that sent him to meet his Maker, that is! In hindsight, this should, perhaps, have served as a warning that less animal fats and more exercise would have been a more prudent regime. Her only regret was that she and

Mossy had never had any children, for if any woman was cut out to spoil a child rotten, it was Martina Clarke. Instead, she took consolation from her only niece, also called Martina, daughter to her sister Mary, and indulged the child shamelessly on her frequent visits to her welcoming kitchen at the parochial house.

There was a certain method in Ma Clarke's madness. She did not approve of these modern "wimmin's libbers," as she described them. They had no idea how the world worked at all, she believed. There was no point in getting up a man's nose by demanding equal this and equal that. All that accomplished was aggravation all round. She was quite happy to be queen of the kitchen, and let the men run the rest of the world. She knew the way to a man's heart. And should the male specimen for whom she was catering not see things the way she did, then there were subtle and more effective ways of achieving the desired objectives.

Thus, when the good Monsignor requested an alteration to the time of his evening repast (the word "meal" would not do it justice), shortly after he arrived in Lahinch, he suddenly found that his morning eggs were unaccountably rock hard, instead of that delicious in-between state of not quite set but not actually runny soft, that allowed a connoisseur to slide the toasted soldiers in without difficulty and get the day off to a good start. His gentle reprimand was rebuffed by claims that the chickens had "gone off" due to being frightened by foxes (only free-range eggs were on offer in the parochial house), and there was nothing the best chef in the county could do about it.

When the buttons on his shirt collars started falling off and took forever to be repaired, it began to dawn on him that all was not right with the world. What broke the poor man's spirit al-

together, though, was when his favourite slippers, the only pair
in years that didn't chafe his bunions, disappeared, and the blame
was attached to a local mongrel that frequented the back door
who was an expert on survival strategies in Lahinch and whose
coat shone like the most pampered thoroughbred in the village,
thanks to Ma Clarke's cordon bleu scraps.

As graciously as he could, he reinstated the old timetable
and, miraculously, the eggs softened, the buttons were repaired
and remained attached indefinitely, and the lost slippers were
"found" at the end of the garden, in remarkably good condition.
Harmony was restored and life went on apace.

Ma Clarke had a small circle of friends, women of her own
vintage, whose children had all grown up and fled the nest, some
of them with great relief. These four ladies could most kindly be
described as "extreme right wing" when it came to matters of faith
and morals. Thus, it should have come as no surprise to anyone
that the movement to abolish, throughout the country, the Saturday evening mass, that currently fulfilled the faithfuls' obliga-
tion "to keep holy the Sabbath Day," should have originated with
this group. This was just the first item on their agenda to reverse
the changes introduced by Vatican II, but it seemed like a good
place to start, given that they had one of their own in a key position to influence events, namely, the PP's housekeeper, Ma Clarke.
Their first tactic was to start referring to the Saturday evening
mass in very disparaging terms, such as the "Golfers' Mass." The
fact that the very same mass was celebrated on Saturday evenings
in nongolfing communities all over the country appeared to have
escaped them. The end justified the means. Propaganda by any
other name would smell just as sweet, they reasoned.

Next, they formed a delegation that consisted of the entire group, less Ma Clarke, to put their case to the Monsignor. No point in revealing their hand too soon, they figured. Of course, no one in the village had the slightest doubt that the PP's housekeeper was in the plot up to her oxters, and developments were awaited with interest.

Pius Ignatious was speechless when he heard their proposition. This reaction alone gave an indication of the seriousness of the matter, for he was a man well-known for pontificating at length on any subject under the sun at the drop of a hat. He muttered some vague promise to consider their proposal and ushered them out of the house as quickly as he could. Then he mopped the cold sweat off his brow. He was between a rock and a hard place and he knew it.

As a former president and still prominent member of the Golf Club, there was no way he could dispense with the Golfers' Mass, and yet he knew that Ma Clarke would wreak terrible havoc with his life if he did not. He sank to his knees in silent supplication. "Oh Lord, help me to bear this cross."

The following Sunday morning, after the usual "Golfers' Mass" on Saturday evening, the eggs went hard again. The poor man groaned. *What next?* he wondered. He hadn't long to wait to find out. His vegetables at lunch were cooked to a mush. His favourite end-piece of the Sunday roast never appeared on his plate. The custard was lukewarm and runny, and the apple tart was short on sugar. The siege had begun.

He decided to consult with Father Malachy. He realised that his Number Two man was not the brightest person in the world, but he knew the village inside out and he had a kind of native cunning that sometimes proved invaluable.

"Get the Bishop to talk to them. Surely they'll respect his word," Father Malachy suggested helpfully.

The idea appealed to the Monsignor. He thought it over for a minute, but then realised that it was impossible. There was no way he could admit that he could not handle the situation. His reputation would be in shreds. They discussed the matter for a few minutes more and then Father Malachy promised to give the matter some further thought and get back to him if he came up with anything. Before he left, Father Malachy broached another subject, one dear to his own heart.

"That little trip to Waterville for the Irish Priests' Golf Society in September, Monsignor. Do you think I could have the extra few days off for that, when the time comes?"

"It's not a good time, Malachy. The tourist season is still going full blast at that time. I don't know how I could manage without you. And you know I'm expecting visitors myself from America around then. I really can't decide just now. I'll have to get this other business out of the way first. Off with you now, and pray for our deliverance."

It was for his local knowledge that I, also, consulted Father Malachy when a competent and pleasant young lady was needed to help in the front office of the golf club for the summer season. He was always most helpful in these situations, but I could not understand the way his face lit up when I mentioned this particular matter to him. When he had calmed down somewhat, he assured me that he had just the girl for the job and not to say a word to anyone else about it for the time being.

He phoned the Monsignor and asked to be invited over for dinner on Monday evening. The Monsignor was perplexed. Did the man not know that he was likely to be served with sautéed slipper in arsenic sauce? Still, he issued the necessary invitation and informed Ma Clarke. She was not amused.

Father Malachy was full of chitchat about the village and the Golf Club when he arrived. The Monsignor usually found this amusing and informative, but on this occasion he was finding it hard to concentrate, and Father Malachy's insights were lost on him. After a little aperitif of sherry, they sat down to the table in the dining room and waited for Ma Clarke to serve their meal. And waited, and waited. Eventually, she appeared and informed them that the timer on the oven was on the blink and the meal would be 20 minutes late. When it did finally appear, it was undercooked and tepid, and not at all appetising. Father Malachy tucked in with gusto, however, and was surprisingly fulsome in his praise for Ma Clarke. The Monsignor was stunned. Had the man taken leave of his senses?

Later, as Ma Clarke cleared the dishes from the table, he leaned over in a conspiratorial fashion to the Monsignor and said, "Do you know that there is a grand handy job going for a bright young lady for the summer at the Golf Club? I was talking to the Manager the other day, and he asked me to recommend someone. Can you think of anyone who might fit the bill?"

As Ma Clarke disappeared from the room, both ears flapping like an African elephant's and being careful not to close the door completely after her, he winked knowingly to the Monsignor. Then the penny dropped. The Mons beamed across at his curate and replied, "Well, Malachy, my boy, I cannot think of anyone off the top of my head, but I'll certainly give the matter some thought. Had you considered anyone in particular yourself?"

"What about Mrs. Clarke's niece? She's about the right age and should be well able to handle anything in that office. Do you think you could ask Mrs. Clarke?"

"Oh dear," replied the Monsignor. "I'm afraid I'm in Mrs. Clarke's bad books at the moment, for some reason. I'm not sure that she'd be interested in helping me out in that or any other matter."

"Well, have a think about it anyway, Monsignor, and if you come up with anything, let me know. Thanks very much for dinner. I must be off now. Got a few jobs to do before turning in for the night." He winked again and went out of the room, being careful to shout his thanks to Ma Clarke in the kitchen before he left.

That good lady was in turmoil in said kitchen. She knew that little Martina would give her eyeteeth for the job in the Golf Club, and her mother would be eternally grateful to her if she swung it for her. But what to do about the "Golfers' Mass"? Matters of principle were at stake here!

The next evening, after work, she hurried off to her group of conspirators to see how the land lay. She heard a progress report from each of them and it was obvious that there was no slackening in their determination to carry on with the campaign. Her heart sank.

"The wonder of it is that those pagan golfers go to mass at all," said Mrs. Quigley. Martina Clarke is nothing if not quick off the mark. She saw her opening and was in like a flash.

"I wonder, ladies, if we wouldn't be condemning some of those poor souls to eternal damnation if we succeeded in getting rid of that 'Golfers' Mass,' after all. I mean, suppose they never went to mass from one end of the year to the other as a result?"

Amid much chewing of tasty fruitcake and slurping of sweet tea, the three other ladies considered the wisdom of what had just been said. Then, in another inspired move, Martina played her ace.

"After all, that John XXIII was a Saint, wasn't he?" There could be no argument with that. Ma Clarke made her way home that evening well satisfied. The "Golfers' Mass" would be spared, but the campaign against Vatican II would continue.

When the Monsignor's eggs arrived the next morning in perfect condition, he thanked God that the siege had been lifted. As the dishes were being cleared after breakfast, he casually mentioned the job at the Golf Club to Ma Clarke and asked for her assistance in tracking down a suitable candidate. Before you could say "Hallelujah," the young Martina was marched into the Monsignor's sitting room for a formal interview and that good man had no hesitation in forming the opinion that she would be eminently suitable for the job. He lost no time in phoning Father Malachy to inform him that he thought he had fortuitously come across just the right candidate for the position, and, by the way, the little matter of Waterville in September did not appear to be a problem after all. Father Malachy was delighted to hear that both matters had been resolved and would be pleased to advise the Golf Club Manager of his good news accordingly.

Life went on apace, and the Golfers' Mass became a fixture in Lahinch.

⚮ May the Best Man Win ⚮

———

SOME GIRLS HAVE it all. Good looks, great figure, brains, personality—the works. Throw in a scratch handicap and international status and it's no wonder that everybody in Lahinch loved Flora Griffin. Including the women! As a golfer she was a stylist, in some contrast to Dily Donworth, the Dame from Dooradoyle, whose swing, after years on the hockey pitch, followed her onto the golf links. A beautiful swinger of the club, Flora hit the ball a long way, effortlessly, and her short game was a joy to behold.

She participated fully in the golfing and social life of the Club and, apart from the odd bit of excusable envy, jealousy, and Irish begrudgery, no one had a bad word to say about her. Some people called her a freak of nature, others put it down to a very firm but loving upbringing by her parents, Michael and Maude, who insisted that she always set high standards for her many talents and never settle for second best. So, after her First Class Honours Degree in Biochemistry at UCC, she went on to do a Masters and then got herself a very good job with a multinational chemical company in Limerick.

Once she had accomplished all that, the matchmakers in the locality got to work. Well, not to work exactly, as they concentrated solely on talking about who might possibly make a good match for her, rather than actually doing anything about it. This suited everyone, for Flora had a mind of her own and was well able to make it up, while the talking matchmakers had none of the diplomatic skills or network of contacts that the real matchmakers of old would have brought to bear on the situation, and were quite content not to meddle.

Speculation was rife that summer as to whether and with whom the lovely Flora might make a move. It was about time for her to settle down and there were three score and ten young men just waiting to make her happy. She was inundated with requests to play in mixed foursomes and had more invitations to socialise than she could accept. In fairness to the girl, it must be said that she spread her favours around a very wide circle, which had the advantage of keeping everybody a little bit happy but nobody completely happy. She carefully withheld the major commitment that they were all seeking.

Toward the end of the summer three main contenders for her hand emerged. The son of the family that owned the chemist's shop in Ennistymon, a hardworking, solid lad who played off a handicap of six, which is very respectable in Lahinch. A doctor from Limerick who had a flourishing practice and now wanted to share it with an appropriate spouse. And Tommy Ryan, the local rich man's son and ne'er-do-well, who had once played to scratch before he discovered booze and girls, in that order, but had never realised his full potential as a golfer, or as a human being, because of his overindulgence in the above.

The chemist's son considered that he had a chance because he had known her since childhood, was a regular partner of hers in mixed foursomes, including the National Mixed Foursomes Competition in which they represented the Club, and because their families were quite close. The doctor considered himself a bit of a catch and could see no reason why the other two would bother to compete with him. Tomser Ryan thought he was God's gift to women and that he had only to exert his not inconsiderable charm and she would fall into his arms, or, preferably, his bed.

When casually questioned about the three boys, or beaux, if you will, Flora declared that she was very fond of the chemist's son, that the doctor would be a fine husband for any girl, and that she had always had a soft spot for Tomser, despite his drinking and womanising, because he made her laugh. Word eventually got back to the lads that there did not seem to be anything in it between them, and this left them in a bit of a quandary. How to bring matters to a head?

In one of those extraordinary coincidences that we all come across in our lives from time to time, the three swains found themselves on the same line of the time sheet for the President's Prize that September. There were dark rumours that Bob Dickins had a hand in this coincidence, in connection with a "book" he might have been running, but discreet, yet very thorough, enquiries failed to establish any truth in them. It appears that our three heroes then decided among themselves that the scores they had that day would determine the order in which they would be allowed a free "run" at endeavouring to get the fair Flora to declare for them.

The doctor agreed reluctantly, because he realised that he was a relative newcomer to the game and, despite his double-digit handicap, would be unlikely to prevail in such a nerve-racking trial. However, he considered his prospects with Flora so good that in the main event he feared no opposition. So Tomser and the chemist's son fought it out. By dint of his greater natural ability, the hours of practice he had put in before he found booze and broads, plus the fact that he had been on the wagon for a whole week before the event, Tomser won the day, although not the President's Prize itself. He had two weeks to make his move.

He tried every trick in the book, but Flora remained adamant throughout. She laughed at his jokes, she delighted in his gifts, she loved his flowers, but every time he tried to get serious she slipped away. He promised to reform, to take the pledge, never to look at another woman, even to take up religion again, but to no avail.

Next up was the chemist's son. His style was altogether more sombre. He was very serious, his manners impeccable, his intentions completely honourable, unlike Tomser, who thought his offer of a few "free samples" might have enhanced his prospects. But, in the end, he too drew a blank.

The final batsman was the good doctor from Limerick. He had the advantage of working in the same town as Flora, well away from the prying eyes of Lahinch. Word got round of dinners in fancy restaurants, rare wines, tuxedos and cocktail dresses. But with the same end result.

The peaceful people of Lahinch were perplexed. Was nobody good enough for the girl?

On the Sunday of the October Bank Holiday weekend, it is traditional in Lahinch to run a Mixed Scramble, with teams of three men and two ladies, and a shotgun start at midday. As there was usually a great and convivial social atmosphere afterward, Monsignor O'Flaherty had prevailed upon the committee some years earlier to hold a charity auction for the local branch of the St. Vincent de Paul Society immediately after the presentation of prizes. This function had now become a fixture and raised considerable funds for that worthy cause. The practice was for members and visitors, and any local traders that could be prevailed upon, to contribute goods or services that could be auctioned off for reasonable sums of money.

Flora played very well for her team and the craic was mighty all the way round. Afterwards, in the bar, they had a few drinks and the laughing and joking continued unabated. Midway through the auction, the auctioneer from Kerry announced that a full set of second-hand ladies' golf clubs, complete with bag and cart, had been donated by Miss Flora Griffin. Amid gasps of amazement, her playing partners enquired what new clubs she was going to get in replacement.

"Oh, I won't be getting a new set," Flora explained.

They were puzzled and went suddenly quiet, waiting for an explanation.

"Well," continued Flora, in a trembling voice, "I won't be needing clubs any more. I've decided to join the Medical Missionaries of Mary, to work as a biochemist in their hospitals in Africa. I'll be leaving on Tuesday."

"But Flora, how could you? You're so gifted in every way!" exclaimed one of her male companions.

"Exactly," replied Flora. "It's payback time."

❧ The Phantom ❧

HE CAME DOWN from the misty hills early every morning, ready
for duty at the Caddiemaster's office before most golfers, except the fanatical few, had set a decent breakfast on their stom-
achs. Not many knew his real name but everyone knew that "The
Phantom" was the best caddie in Lahinch. Tall, gaunt, and pale,
despite his outdoor lifestyle, his most notable feature was his
silence. Hence his nickname.

Bob Dickins, the Caddiemaster, fully appreciated the treasure that he had available to him and husbanded him carefully,
with the result that they both made a good living out of it. Bob
reserved him for only the best customers and they, for the most
part, showed their appreciation by means of generous tips. He
was always careful to explain that The Phantom was a man of
few words, but even this was an exaggeration, for the truth was
that The Phantom was a man of no words. His great gift was
that he could assess a total stranger's ability to hit the ball after

only a few shots and thereafter club him to perfection in all but the most extreme conditions, given only the player's reasonable cooperation. He felt, or at least it was assumed that he felt — for he never bothered to confide in anyone — that words were superfluous to the playing of the great game and that all that was required was total concentration and dedication. If the truth be known, he was probably right, because he caddied for some of the greatest players in the country when they came to Lahinch and they invariably did very well under his guidance. His knowledge of the greens was legendary and it was said in the snugs of the village that he could guide a blind man into the hole.

An English gentleman, Rupert St. John Winterman, once entered the South of Ireland, an open match play championship, to show the Irish a thing or two. In fairness to the man, it must be said that he phoned the Secretary/Manager some months beforehand, at the time he sent in his entry, to enquire about booking the services of the best caddie in the place, and Bob Dickins was persuaded to commit the services of The Phantom when the words "money no object" were used. Loyalty to regulars was all very well, but if the best caddie was booked months in advance, what could a man do?

Rupert St. John arrived three days in advance of the tournament to get to know the course, but was unable to use the services of The Phantom because that good man's diary was chockablock and he had only booked him for the tournament proper. Thus on the Sunday morning, when the better players first get involved in the matches, they met as strangers on the first tee. Bob had been at pains to explain to Mr. Winterman that his caddie was not gifted in the verbal department but that he understood the Queen's English very well and responded to the title "Caddie."

"Well, my good man," said Rupert St. John on the tee before they set off, "I understand that I am to refer to you as 'Caddie'. You may call me 'Sir' if you need to draw my attention to anything. Right ho?" And off they went.

It is to The Phantom's everlasting credit that not one "Sir" passed his lips in all the holes he carried that man's bag. However, he did not allow Rupert St. John's patronising attitude to interfere in any way with his professionalism as a caddie. He brought him all the way to the semifinals that year and earned tremendous respect from both the player himself and the cognoscenti in the galleries that followed them.

Then they came to the fifteenth hole all flat in the semifinal. Two good drives into a gentle, northerly breeze, for the Old Lady was in benign humour that day, and his opponent was "away" first by a margin of no more than a yard or two. Under increasing pressure, the young Irish lad from Dublin put his ball in the middle of the green but not near the pin.

"What do you think, Caddie?" Rupert St. John enquired of The Phantom, although by now he had enough sense not to expect an answer. The Phantom handed him a 6-iron, the distance to the pin being 170 yards. Rupert St. John looked at the club in his hand, looked at the 165-yard marker some way ahead and said, "I'm sorry, my good man, but for the first time in four days I must beg to differ. 170 yards into a breeze, slightly uphill ... I have to go for the 5-iron."

The Phantom appeared not to have heard what had been said and didn't move a muscle. Rupert St. John replaced the 6-iron in

the bag himself and took out the 5. He proceeded to blast the
ball over the back of the green, having failed to take account of
the adrenaline pumping through his veins at that stage of a vital
match. He then chipped too hard, ran six feet past the pin and
failed to hole the putt. The lad from Dublin holed out in two.
Rupert St. John was numerically only one down with three holes
still to play, but his fate was sealed and everyone knew it. His
opponent put him under further pressure by putting his tee shot
at the sixteenth par 3 to within five yards of the pin. St. John
tried to steer the ball toward the hole instead of swinging the
club head through it, left the ball short of the green, and failed
once again to get down in two. It was all over then. It is not often
that a man comes back from dormie two down in the semifinal
match of the "South."

Fair dues to Rupert St. John Winterman, he took it like a
man and gave Bob a handsome sum for his services, a large part
of which found its way to The Phantom.

After the match, Bob enquired gently of The Phantom, as
they shared a cuppa in Bob's office, a rare privilege for a caddie,

"What went wrong with yer Englishman?"

The Phantom took a mouthful of his tea, gazed off into the
distance and said quietly, "He played with his head, instead of
his heart."

Some weeks later a letter arrived addressed to "The Phantom, c/o Lahinch Golf Club, County Clare, Ireland." Inside,
folded in a sheet of richly grained paper, were six 10-pound notes.
On the paper were four typed words but no signature.

It was a six.

❧ Jack the Lad ❧

――――――――

THERE WERE MANY big men in County Clare, but Jack Kenefick
was one of the biggest. It wasn't just his size that impressed
people either, for Jack had "presence." He was the first man you
saw when you entered a room full of people, the centre of any
crowd on the sideline of a football match, no matter where he
sat, and, in his younger days, the player around whom every football game revolved, no matter which position he played.

As his footballing days were ending he took up golf and became quite addicted, as had many before him. He never really
accepted that he could not dominate that little white ball as he
had its larger, leather counterpart. It took him some considerable time to realise that mastering the little ball required many
skills, and that no one yet in the history of the game of golf had
been blessed with all of them. However, he persevered to such
an extent that he made the Senior Cup Team in Lahinch on two
occasions, but the effort needed to retain his place proved to be

unacceptable, and he settled for more sociable golf at a lower level.

In fact, he found this level of golf much more enjoyable and, after a stint on the Junior Cup Team, he settled down to become a stalwart on the Bruen Shield Panel. He became a popular member of the OGS—the Oldest Golfing Society—and, in every sense, was the essence of a Real Golfer. He never missed his weekend singles on a Saturday and four-ball on a Sunday. He was fond of his pint, but did not drink to excess, as this could not be reconciled with giving the game his best effort. He loved the cut and thrust of the national competitions when they came around each year in the spring and summer. He was so totally absorbed in sport that he had never had time to get serious enough about a girl to get married.

Then his back let him down. Damaged ligaments in his lower back were a legacy of his footballing days. They did not bother him generally, but, with advancing years, the extra weight around his middle and too many wettings in the winter, they were becoming a problem. One Saturday morning they screamed in protest as he bent down to retrieve a ball from the hole on the practice putting green. His back muscles went into spasm to protect the injured parts as he sank in a very undignified way to his knees. His friends burst into heartless laughter when they came upon him in this position and gave him a hard time about praying for inspiration to save the money they were going to play for. It took some time to convince them that he was, in fact, in real difficulty and even then, as they roughly lifted him back onto his feet, they were still chuckling at the sight of the big man humbled.

They dumped him unceremoniously in the lounge upstairs and advised him to ease the pain with some of the best Irish whiskey on the premises as soon as the staff arrived for work. Mrs. Casey, the Catering Manageress, took pity on him when she opened up the restaurant about half an hour later and fed him several Irish Coffees, using liberal quantities of her secret stash of whiskey to give the coffee the necessary numbing effect.

By the time his erstwhile friends returned from their round, Big Jack was feeling no pain at all. So much so, in fact, that they had to arrange for him to be transported home in the back of a flatbed truck, as there was no way the man could bend his body in and out of a more conventional vehicle.

He did not improve much in the following weeks and eventually, with great reluctance, he was obliged to take his friends' advice and make an appointment with Dr. Joe Moore. Dr. Joe was very sympathetic but could not entirely hide his amusement at the helplessness of the big man.

"I'll give you something to ease the discomfort and you should sleep on a very hard surface for a while. The floor, if possible. However, this little problem will not go away by itself. It will need a little help."

He wrote out the name and address of a physiotherapy clinic in Limerick and gave it to Jack. Why did he pick this particular one? Only God knows!

Jack made an appointment and managed to turn up on time. He found that it was quite a busy practice, with about a dozen private cubicles and four physiotherapists, who were kept going most of the time.

"Mr. Cusack is off sick today," the receptionist told him, "so Miss Heggarty will see you instead. Number six, down the hallway, on the right."

Jack became uneasy as he made his way down the hallway. Miss Heggarty? He didn't fancy that. A Mr. Cusack was one thing but a Miss Heggarty was quite another. Jack lost his nerve halfway down the hallway and turned quickly on his heel, with the intention of coming back another day when Mr. Cusack returned to his full health. However, he failed to complete the manoeuvre, as his back protested in the only way it could, by seizing up again and, in the process, dumping him on his knees on the floor.

Several pairs of helping hands were immediately at his side and he found himself gently but firmly eased into Cubicle Number 6 and the tender mercies of Miss Catriona Heggarty. She gave him a few minutes to compose himself and then inquired as to the origins of his ailment. Jack looked with a jaundiced eye at the young lady asking the questions and gave the necessary responses with ill grace. He felt like a trapped animal and cooperated only because he knew he would be unable to get out of there under his own steam.

Cathy eventually persuaded him to strip to his underwear so that she could assess the damage to his back. Jack had never felt so humiliated in his life. The fact that he could hardly carry out any of the manoeuvers that she requested further annoyed him, forgetting that it was for the purpose of making an assessment that they were requested, not as some form of demonstration of manly prowess.

She managed to get him onto the padded table and proceeded to give him the full treatment for the next three-quarters of an hour. The poor man was twisted and contorted into positions that the Holy Inquisition would have been proud of. At one stage the slip of a girl was actually kneeling on his back, pressing with all her might on his lower spine. In total mortification, Jack prayed that this would never get out or he would not be able to show his face in Lahinch again.

When she had finished her angelic ministrations, she suggested, as tactfully as possible, that the loss of some weight from around his middle would aid the recovery process. Jack was dumbstruck and could only manage a mumbled response.

Finally, to finish off the session, he was given Ultrasonic and Interferential treatments, which he found not at all unpleasant. He was able to dress himself afterward by going about it very slowly and carefully, and he actually managed to walk to the reception area without help. With a sheepish grin, he paid for the session, made an appointment for two days hence and went on his way. Compared to his recent efforts at walking, he practically skipped along the pavement to his car. He had not felt such freedom of movement for weeks. As he drove back to Lahinch, he couldn't get one thought out of his mind, no matter how hard he tried: the young lady had lovely warm hands. To his surprise and consternation, he could not wait to get back to Limerick for his next appointment.

It is not unusual in healer/patient relationships for the one receiving the treatment to develop a mild crush on the one giving it, when opposite sexes are involved. Thus it was with Jack. Golf was ruled out for the time being, so all he had to occupy his mind was work, and the lovely Miss Catriona Heggarty. Twelve more sessions followed in the ensuing weeks, until the day came when she told him he was on his own. He had his exercises to do daily and should just be careful how he treated his back, especially in wet or cold weather. He was very sad as he left the clinic for the last time.

Jack got back to his golf soon after that, although he was careful not to overdo it. To his surprise, he found he was playing quite well, as the layoff had sharpened his concentration. The work on his back, his new diet, plus the exercises he was now doing regularly had helped his swing a lot. Things might have returned to normal, had Fate not intervened once again.

This time it was the Lady Captain's doing. She accosted Jack as he returned from a light session over at the practice ground by the Castle Course one Sunday afternoon.

"Ah, Jack, the very man. I have an emergency and you must help me out. I have invited a guest to play in the mixed foursomes this afternoon, but the partner I had arranged for her has just phoned to say he can't make it. Death in the family, or something. Would you ever be a dear man and stand in instead? I'd be so grateful."

Jack huffed and puffed for a while, trying to think of an acceptable excuse to refuse the Lady Captain. Mixed foursomes were not his bag at all. What would the lads say? Just as he was about to utter some outrageous lie to extricate himself from his predicament, he was amazed to hear the dulcet tones of none other than Miss Catriona Heggarty behind him.

"Now, Jack Kenefick, after all I've done for you, the least you can do is play one round with me." She put her hand possessively on his back and gave it a little rub.

Poor old Jack was lost there and then. Not only did he play that round with her, he played many more rounds besides, in between having their four children over the next 10 years. It seems that the bigger they are, the harder they fall, after all!

⚘ Having Your Cake ⚘

———

Ellen glanced at her husband's Callaway golf clubs in the hallway, the ones that she had recently polished, and thought of the lovely Sue.

Mr. Jim was in for a bit of a surprise. This would be the last evening for a while that he would walk jauntily up the road swinging his briefcase. His comfortable little world was about to wobble on its axis. Unless he was sensible, of course. She looked at her own set of clubs further down the hallway and smiled grimly to herself. She hadn't used them much this past summer but she was certainly going to use them now!

As Jim opened the front door, the rich aroma of spaghetti in Bolognese sauce filled his nostrils and he sighed with pleasurable anticipation. Subconsciously, his mind registered the shine on his golf clubs as he passed them in the hall on his way to greet his wife, now dutifully preparing his dinner tray in the kitchen.

"Hard day, darling?" Ellen asked

"Oh, not so bad," he said, pecking her on the cheek.

"Go on in and watch the telly for yourself. I'll have your dinner ready in a moment. Would you like a glass of red wine with the Bolognese?"

"Lovely, pet. Thank you."

He sauntered into the living room, where he was accustomed to have his evening meal ensconced in front of the TV with his feet up, beside the coal fire.

Ellen brought in the aromatic meal and the promised wine on a tray and placed it carefully on his lap. Then she brought in her own and sat on the sofa next to his chair. She had arranged for the three children to be with friends for an hour or two, so they had this time for themselves. She chatted about inconsequential things for a few minutes and then, casually, as if an afterthought, asked, "When were you thinking of hopping off to Spain with your golfing buddies this autumn, darling?"

"October, I suppose. Same as last year."

"I think that's wonderful. You always come back so refreshed after that trip. It really does you a power of good to get away from it all before the bad weather sets in. Cuts down on colds and flu too, don't you think, darling?"

"You're quite right, my pet, it certainly does." He smiled contentedly at the thought.

"Henry Power called earlier, by the way. He wondered if you were OK for the long golfing weekend in Killarney again this year."

"You wouldn't mind, dear, would you? We do a lot of business with old Henry."

"Not at all, darling. Needs must. I'll have Mother over while you're gone and she'll be great company."

They watched the TV for a short while in companionable quiet, listening to the evening news with the volume just high enough to hear but not so high as to interfere with conversation. Her heart began to pound just a little as she waited for the right moment. Then she decided.

"Darling, I've great news for you, too. I've decided to play with you in the mixed foursomes next weekend."

He paused for a moment before replying, gathering his thoughts at this unexpected turn in the conversation. "That's lovely, pet, but..."

"No 'buts', darling. I'm playing with you."

The honey trap snapped shut.

She concentrated on her plate of food for the next few minutes, knowing that this was the critical moment in her strategy. He could only play with one partner.

He slowly began to chew his food again as he considered his predicament. He thought of the lovely Sue. And all the trouble she could bring down on his head. His mind went back to the moment he had entered the house. His home where he was king, cosseted and comforted to his heart's desire, with almost unlimited time to play golf.

He wasn't fool enough to think that this was just about the mixed foursomes next weekend. He realised that a gauntlet had been thrown down and he had to make a choice. His mind wandered to the set of new Callaways in the hallway, the best clubs that money could buy, and how they had transformed his game.

He savoured the fine food in his mouth and eyed the rich red of the wine in his glass. He thought about Killarney and Spain.

"Certainly, dear, if that's what you want. I'll make the necessary arrangements tomorrow."

Now it was his turn to concentrate on his plate. Ellen glanced sideways at him and, satisfied that she had made her point and won, smiled inwardly to herself.

Her Bolognese had never tasted so good.

❧ MAD MAX ❧

———

I BREEZED INTO the bar, as is my wont, to deliver the mail one quiet Thursday and greeted the solitary member, solemnly sucking a sad pint, gazing sightlessly out toward Liscannor.

"Cheer up, Max, it might never happen," I said gently.

He looked at me gloomily. "It already has."

I hesitated before asking the next, obvious question, as I knew from experience that it could be decidedly dangerous to get involved with members' stories. Some of them have been known to last for hours! Max was a decent old skin, however, so I decided to risk it.

"What's that, then?" I asked, giving him the opening he needed.

He drank deeply from his pint, looked me in the eye and said, slowly and clearly, so that there could be no misunderstanding, "My caddiecar has gone mad."

This is where the truly gifted Secretary/Manager comes into his own, for the wrong reaction could make an enemy for life, whereas the right one could gain an ally forever. Tact, diplomacy, and the utmost sensitivity are called for. So, instead of laughing in his face, tipping his pint over his head and walking out of the bar, I glanced around swiftly to ensure that no one was looking and that I was not being set up, leaned an elbow gently on the brass rail of the counter and made a noncommittal noise in my throat, guaranteed not to offend but offering just a hint of encouragement.

"I know you probably think I'm dotty, but I swear that the damned thing has a mind of its own. It's electric, you know."

Still not sure which way the wind was blowing and beginning to wish that I had not offered a sympathetic ear, I nodded sagely and made another noncommittal throat noise. He took this for encouragement and launched into his story.

"I bought it secondhand recently from the local pro-shop. I was delighted with the price, which was modest for such a slightly used cart, less than a year old, but I think now that that old guy knew more than he was letting on when he sold it to me.

"Things went fine for a couple of weeks and the relief to my auld back was great. I certainly didn't feel half as tired after a round as I used to. Then one day some of my buddies were kidding me about it and asked why I had given in to 'Anno Domini' and bought an electric cart. Joining in the spirit of the occasion, I said that I got it 'because of the muddy-maroon colour which would go with the state of my trousers over the winter season.'

"This raised a bit of a laugh from the lads, but the damned thing must have overheard the remark because, two days later out on the course, I stopped the cart and went forward just a bit to identify a ball that I thought was mine. I was bending over, trying to see the number, when I heard the wheezing, clicking noise the monster makes when it's moving. I turned my head slightly and saw it, out of the corner of my eye, bearing down on me. I spun on my good leg out of the way, just in time."

He paused while he took another swig of his pint, looked me in the eye and dared me to question his version of events.

"You must have left it with the power slightly on," I couldn't help remarking.

"Nope. Switch was off."

There was no answer to that, so I tried to dismiss it by saying "Surely, one little incident..."

"Aye," he agreed, "one little incident doesn't mean anything. But how do you explain this? Two weeks later I was playing with some of the lads and one of them was slagging me about the cart. He called it 'a mobile Zimmer frame.' Ten minutes later I let it off to freewheel down a slight hill well away from where he was walking ahead of me, when the damned thing turned left and tried to ram him. Fortunately, it missed him and hit his pull cart. He had to replace one of the wheels afterward."

"Aw, now, Max, everybody knows those things are always biased in one direction or the other."

He raised his head slowly and stared at Liscannor Head for a full five seconds before answering. A slight shiver ran down his body as he said, in a very quiet voice, "Three holes later it did the same thing, only this time it turned to the right. Bill still has a plaster cast around his ankle."

I could see that the man was upset, but a few coincidences like that would hardly be sufficient cause. He looked at me and could see that I clearly did not believe him. He went on.

"The next weekend was wet and at the twelfth hole, the point furthest from the clubhouse, just after I had criticised it because its wheels were slipping on the wet grass, it stopped dead and refused to move another inch."

"That must have been inconvenient," I sympathised. "It would be a hell of a job pushing one of those things back from there in the rain. Wouldn't help your golf, or your back. How did you get out of it?"

A ghost of a smile crossed his face.

"I threatened not to plug it into the mains when we got home."

"Good for you," I laughed, and made to leave the bar. He put his hand on my sleeve and said, "But that's not all."

I had been afraid of that. I had hoped to complete some work that afternoon for the Honorary Treasurer, who was inclined to become a bit tetchy toward the end of the month, but that plan was out the window now. In any case, Max's need appeared to be greater.

"I lent it to my best friend, Joe Walsh. He was considering getting one and wanted a trial."

He paused dramatically and, looking me straight in the eye, he continued, "I visited him in the hospital shortly afterwards and asked what had happened. It seems he was critical of it after the first two holes because it was not going fast enough. He said to his playing partner that he would make sure to get a modern, high-tech model, and not somebody else's hand-me-down. Once he told me that, I knew he would have had to pay a price. The machine jammed in high speed for the rest of the round and by the time he got to the eighteenth it brought on a mild

heart attack. He has sworn off the idea for life and hasn't spoken to me since he got out of the hospital.

"I forgot to plug it into the mains to recharge it before I
next used it, but, do you know what? It ran for the full round
without the charge-up. I just can't understand it. Poor Joe! I
hope he makes a full recovery."

This was fascinating. I should have tried harder to make my
escape and get back to the Treasurer's figures, but I had to hear
the end of the story. So, God forgive me, I encouraged him.

"Is that it?"

"No," he sobbed, "there's more. A week after Joe came out of
hospital, one of the greenkeepers passed me by on the course on
a brand new Ransome ride-on, greens-cutting machine. He called
out as he passed, "Why don't you get yourself a decent machine
like this, while you're at it?" and he laughed. The monster gave a
couple of loud wheezes and made some teeth-watering, gear-
grinding noises. Five holes further on we met the new machine
again, travelling between greens. Didn't mine make a beeline for
it! And the Ransome four times bigger! The greenkeeper swerved
to avoid a collision and ended up going out of control on the side
of a dune. The result? £946.83 worth of damage to the machine
and three weeks off work for yer man with a strained back."

"I remember that! Dan Scuffins, wasn't it? He hasn't got up
on a machine since," I said, amazed.

He looked at me knowingly.

"There's worse. It attacked my wife."

"Oh, my God. What happened?"

"Well," he said, warming to his theme now, "I keep it in the
garden shed, because she insisted that 'she would not have that

muck spreader in the house'. I pleaded with her to keep her voice down, but she only looked at me oddly and snorted self-righteously. I worried about that for a while, but nothing happened, so I forgot about it. Then one day she was putting out the washing on the line while I was doing a bit of clearing out in the shed. I laid everything out carefully on the grass, including the cart, but in two pieces and without the battery, which was inside the house plugged into the mains. I swear to God, didn't the part with the motor and wheels get between her and the basket and, when she backed away from the washing line to pick up something else, she tripped over it and sprained her arm. I had to do the housework for a fortnight afterward."

I could take no more.

"Aw, come on, Max. Each one of those dramas could have a perfectly simple, logical explanation."

He climbed slowly down off the barstool, drew himself up to his full five feet four inches, and said with conviction, "Yes, but could they all be explained together?"

There was no answer to that. He shuffled forlornly out of the bar and I returned to the safety of my bookkeeping.

✤ Hot Stuff! ✤

NOVEMBER IS FREQUENTLY unfriendly to golfers. It can rain, it can blow, and it can freeze. However, despite years of experience to the contrary, they always hope that November will be a fine, dry month, with four perfect weekends for outdoor activities and several sparkling Wednesdays for those fortunate enough to be able to play midweek.

So, when the last Saturday of November had deteriorated into a bitterly cold, frost-filled night of sparkling blackness, Bob Dickins was not surprised to find himself all alone in his Starter's Office the following Sunday morning, with the unfamiliar glare of the frosty fairways causing some little discomfort to his eyes. The course was closed and, if the cold snap persisted, it could run into days before play would be allowed again.

But guess what? Some dozen or so hard-core optimists actually turned up, in the forlorn hope that a miracle would happen and the sun and the Gulf Stream would banish Jack Frost and all his nasty doings in time for a few holes before dusk. In addition, several cars cruised slowly past the entrance with all heads turned to see if there was any prospect of a thaw, although they hadn't the nerve to go against ordinary common sense and actually turn into the car park, as this would imply a degree of hope that would put Gamblers Anonymous to shame. To judge these simpletons with a degree of fairness, one should allow that much of their behaviour was force of habit, and that their cars nearly started automatically at a fixed hour every weekend and headed along the same route to the same destination, regardless of the circumstances. Thus, they didn't really expect the course to be playable; they were merely doing what they do every weekend, heading down to the Club. Mind you, when they come all the way from Limerick, one has to wonder.

Around midmorning, Bob decided that it was time to break the monotony by going upstairs in the clubhouse for a hot cuppa and one of Mrs. Casey's scrumptious buttered scones. His brain was in neutral, he was content with life, and the only slightly bothersome matter that required his attention was whether or not to take a bit of a winter break before things got going again in the spring. He mulled over this profound problem as the steaming tea and the butter-dripping scone were delivered to his favourite table at the far end of the lounge, the one over-looking the third green and the Atlantic Ocean.

As he was pouring the first and best cup of tea from the pot, one of the lads from Limerick sitting at a nearby table enquired of him, "Bob, did you see Dan McQuaid at all this morning? We had a tentative arrangement to play with him."

In an absentminded sort of way, Bob replied, "Yes, he shoved his head into my office earlier to say he wasn't staying. He'd decided to bring his cattle up onto the hills of the Burren for the winter instead." He turned back to the task in hand.

After a moment's silence, the Limerick lads hooted with laughter and one of them cried out, "For God's sake, Bob, can't you answer a simple question without taking the piss?"

Bob looked up, startled.

"What do you mean? I did answer your question!"

"Come on, Bob, we know it's a quiet Sunday and you have nothing better to do than ballhop a couple of city boys for the amusement of the local populace."

"I'm sorry, lads, did I miss something? You asked me a simple question and I gave you a simple answer. What's the problem?" Bob took a bite out of the dripping scone and munched contentedly.

Another silence while the Limerick lads contemplated the situation and surveyed the room to see if they were being set up for anything. Since no one could figure out what exactly was bothering them, they were met with blank stares, which irritated them even more.

"For the love of Mike, give us a break. What eejit would bring cattle up into the hills in the winter and keep them on the lowlands in the summer? Do you think there are no farmers in County Limerick?"

Bob's brain clicked into top gear immediately. He continued to munch on the mouthful of scone while he assessed the situation. Eventually, he said, half apologetically, "God, lads, I'm sure that's what he said. Honest!"

But the Limerick lads were having none of it. One of them reached into his back pocket and pulled out a wad of notes. Throwing three of the notes onto the table, he followed the gesture with a challenge.

"I've got 30 quid that says he will most definitely not bring his cattle up onto the high hills of the Burren for the winter. Now, Bob Dickins, put up or shut up!"

"Lads, lads! This isn't a betting matter. I only said what the man told me. Now, it's the day of rest. Why don't you let the matter be and allow a man to enjoy his cuppa in peace?"

The Limerick lads could smell blood now and there was no way they would back off. They looked at each other knowingly and nodded. Each one then pulled out his money from wherever on his person he kept it and they made a neat pile in the middle of the table. One of them counted it.

"Well, now, Mr. Bob Dickins. You've had your fun at our expense long enough. Time to pay the piper. Retract that ridiculous statement or match this 500 pounds."

Bob took another bite of scone and a big swallow of tea while he contemplated their faces in silence. Around the room some knowing looks appeared on local faces. But not a word was spoken.

Finally, Bob announced, "I don't think I have that kind of money on me," and he looked around helplessly.

"Never mind that. Can't you borrow a few quid from your buddies? Don't you Lahinch guys always stick together?"

"Lord, no. I'd never borrow money to bet with. But maybe some of the lads would like to make up the difference themselves? I can manage 300 of my own."

The three Limerick lads glared around the room.

"Well, any takers?"

Silence.

"What? Have ye left all yer balls at home, lads? How did ye expect to play golf without balls! Is there not a man amongst the lot of ye?"

After a long pause, a 50-pound note appeared on the table from the left wing. Three more followed, slowly, from various parts of the room until the total of 500 was reached.

Bob finished off his scone, handed his 300 to the barman who was holding the wager and said quietly, "Follow me, lads."

The whole company trooped out of the bar and down to the car park after him, leaving the bemused barman with a thousand quid to mind on this very slack Sunday. They split into small groups, piled into several cars and headed off north toward the Burren where Dan McQuaid had his smallholding. Within 20 minutes they arrived and enquired of the lady of the house as to the whereabouts of her husband. She was perplexed at the unexpected arrival of so many people and, although it was well away from the poteen season, feared something was amiss. This made her somewhat reluctant to reveal his whereabouts. Bob explained briefly that they were friends of his from the Golf Club and they needed to consult with him on an important matter. At this, the good woman relented and pointed the way to where her husband could be found.

The little group set off and some 30 minutes later came across the very Dan McQuaid himself, sitting on a rock, puffing on his pipe. Thirty-five fine head of cattle, watched over by an alert black-and-white collie dog, were munching the tender grass, which surprisingly was not frozen. The first subconscious alarm bell should have gone off in the minds of the Limerick lads, but it didn't. They were so sure they were right that they just wanted confirmation from their friend Dan and to celebrate their victory over Bob Dickins. Sunday wouldn't be a write-off after all, as far as they were concerned.

"Dan! The very man!" cried the instigator of the bet. "Would you settle an argument for us? Are you taking these cattle up or down the hill?" Dan looked at them as if they were mad.

"Up the bloody hill, ye blind eejit! What do you think I'm doing?"

The Limerick lads were stunned and the locals let out loud guffaws at their discomfiture.

"Up the hill? For what? It's the start of winter. Shouldn't they be put indoors?"

Dan McQuaid looked around and twigged what was happening. He took his Limerick friend by the arm, led him gently to a rock and sat him down.

"Open your mouth and blow softly out," he instructed. The man did so and the misty breath drifted upward.

"Now, ye great big city slicker, why did your breath rise?"

"I dunno. Why?"

"Because it's hotter than the air outside your body, and hot air rises. In fact, all heat rises. So, the limestone rocks of the Burren absorb heat throughout the summer. This heat rises through the rocks in the winter, making it warmer at the top of the hills than the bottom. Hence, there is better grazing on the hills in the winter than there is on the lowlands."

He took a big suck on his pipe and blew out a cloud of smoke to demonstrate his point once more. Then, with a big grin on his face, he said, "I suppose Mr. Dickins here has cleaned ye out again? Holy God, some people never learn. Bob, I'll be having a very large whiskey on you the next time I'm in the Club bar. Good luck, lads!"

"And while you're enjoying that whiskey, Dan," Bob said, "I'll be somewhere sampling sun, sand, sangria, and something else which I can't recall just now."

He would take a little winter holiday for himself after all.

◆ GORGEOUS GUSSIE ◆

———

THE BOY WALKED dejectedly along the road. The puppy bounced along by his side, big black ears flapping, without a care in the world. It was a case of "ignorance is bliss" because that little puppy did not know the trouble they were heading for, whereas the boy did. His father would blow a fuse when he arrived home with another mouth to feed. His Da had been out of work for two years now and times were hard in the Curley household at Number 16, Mahony Terrace, Lahinch.

Tim Curley was 12 years old and had never owned anything of any significance in his short life, apart from the clothes he stood up in. And those did not amount to much. He only had the use of them until he outgrew them and would then pass them on to his younger brother—just as they had been passed to him by his older brother. You could say he had a leasehold interest in the clothes. So, when the man had offered the puppy for sale for only a pound, provided it got a good home, Tim could not resist the bargain. He reasoned that God must have made him save that pound, which had been burning a hole in his pocket for the last three weeks, for this moment. Why else had he resisted all the other temptations that come the way of a 12-year-old with money in his pocket? They were meant to be together.

While this explanation seemed perfectly reasonable to Tim, as he trudged ever more slowly homeward, he knew that his parents would be much harder to convince. His Da in particular. His Ma he thought he could get around, but his Da was definitely going to be a challenge. He gave a little shudder of fearful anticipation as he opened the creaky gate at the front of Number 16 and went in.

The reception to his announcement that he had bought a dog was much as he had expected, only worse. His father raged and ranted and threatened all sorts of retribution. His mother cried. He was told to get rid of the dog or sleep with it in the back shed. He retreated, supperless, to the cold and draughty shed, dismayed but undaunted in his determination to hold on to his new bosom buddy. Gussie, part sheepdog, part spaniel and part unknown, was a black-and-white mutt that now belonged to him.

After dark, his mother came out to the shed with something for him to eat and drink. She gave him a hug and patted the dog but told him that they had no way of feeding it, the way things were. She cried again before she left them to their cold and lonely vigil.

The next morning, he awoke with the birds and the dawn. The boy and the dog struggled out of their uncomfortable bed on the floor of the shed and tumbled into the morning dew. He knew it was very early, for there was nothing else stirring in the back gardens of Mahony Terrace. He decided not to approach the house for the time being, lest he cause more trouble by waking people before they were ready. He quietly played with the puppy instead. The dog was about six months old, with a white flash across its nose, one white foot and white all over its tummy (which Tim had already discovered it liked to have tickled).

He found an old golf ball in the shed and they started to play with that. The dog took to the game like a duck to water. Tim threw the ball, the dog chased after it and brought it back to be thrown again. On one occasion, Tim threw it to the end of what passed for a garden, and it hopped into the long grass that featured prominently in the layout. He held onto the dog until the ball had disappeared from sight and then released him. He chased off merrily after the ball and, having sniffed around for a moment or two, easily located it in the long grass. He brought it straight back to his new young master and dropped the ball at Tim's feet. Tongue hanging out, head cocked to one side, he stood waiting for more fun and games. Tim had a flash of inspiration.

Later on in the morning, he knocked timidly at the kitchen door and asked for his breakfast. His mother hauled him in by the shirt and told him to wash before sitting down to eat. His father glowered at him from his place at the top of the table. Things seemed to have cooled down a bit, he thought as he washed. Maybe his Ma had "worked on" his Da in the mysterious way that mothers have, and he might be able to keep Gussie after all.

The meal was silent, as none of the children wanted to bring the wrath of their father down on their heads in his present humour. When they had finished eating, they scampered from the room lest any trouble, not of their making, should befall them. It was one thing to be belted for something you had done yourself, but to share someone else's trouble was not on.

"Let's have a look at the mongrel," his father growled when they had all gone.

"Promise you won't hurt him?"

"I won't hurt him. Bring him in here for a minute."

Tim ran to the shed and picked up the dog.

"You be good now, and don't do anything to make him mad," he pleaded with the mutt.

He marched proudly back to the kitchen and placed the mutt on the floor in front of his father. The man stroked him gently, remembering days long gone when his best friend was a dog not unlike this one, only white with liver-coloured patches.

The dog reared up on its hind legs playfully and the man jumped up, swearing.

"It's a bloody bitch! The eejit was sold a bitch. We'll have some time around here when she comes into heat. Is that a fool you're raisin' there, Missus. Doesn't he know the difference? Oh, God, preserve us from all harm!"

And with that, he stormed out of the house. Tim looked bewildered. The man who had sold him Gussie had called him a dog. How come "he" was now a "she"? He'd never hear the end of this. He reckoned any chance he had of keeping it now was gone. To his surprise, his mother pulled him to her and gave him a hug.

"Never mind, son, we'll get her fixed somehow when the time comes. And don't worry about her name. "Gorgeous Gussie" was

a famous lady tennis player long ago, so we'll say she's called after her. Now, before you go out to play, there are a few rules you
will have to keep, if you want to hold on to that mutt. She eats
only scraps and leftovers. If I catch you taking good food from
the kitchen for her, she's out, and you'll not be far behind. Second, you clean up her mess until she's house-trained. I had
enough of all that with you lot. Third, if there's any trouble with
the neighbours, she goes. Finally, when you're at school she stays
in the backyard or the shed. Not in the house! Understood? Now,
scat with you, before I change my mind."

Tim was out of the kitchen like a prisoner out of jail, the
dog running along behind. She had already decided who her boss
was in this household. They ran up the road, where Tim went
into a small shop and bought a cheap packet of biscuits with his
remaining few pence. Then they set off for the beach, where he
was going to put his plan into operation.

Over the next few weeks, Tim spent hours with the dog,
practising and practising. Things were still difficult at home, his
father never having really forgiven him for bringing home a bitch.
He was glad of the pleasure and companionship of the dog away
from the house. About four weeks later he set off one morning,
again with a packet of cheap biscuits in his pocket, for the golf
links, keeping his fingers crossed that his little plan would work.

He picked his spot on the links carefully because he had been
there before with some of his friends and knew his way around.
He gave the young dog a command and she started hunting
around, sniffing everywhere. Then she dived into a clump of grass
and came out with a golf ball held gently in her velvety mouth.
She brought it to Tim and dropped it at his feet and he gave her

a piece of biscuit as a reward. He patted her gratefully on the head and started her searching again. They spent the next two hours on the golf course, searching for balls and finding quite a few.

Eventually tiring of the task, he made his way toward the Pro Shop with his treasures and went in to Old Walter Partridge. Walter knew the score with Tim's family and, although it went against the grain, he was very generous with his price for the golf balls. Tim came out beaming, a crisp new note in his hand, and he set off, heart singing, his plan a success, to tell his Ma the good news.

He burst in the back door, shouting, "Ma, Ma, look what I've got," and he planked the 20-pound note on the table. His mother looked at it in amazement and then, for no apparent reason, gave him a clip on the ear that sent him spinning.

"Ahhh, Ma!" Tim wailed. "What did ya do that for?"

"Where did you get that money?" she demanded. "If you've been thievin', I'll flay you alive!"

His father, sitting in the corner reading yesterday's paper that a kindly neighbour had sent in, added in a threatening voice, "Where did ya get that money? Have you been thieving with some of them other brats from the end of the street?"

"No, Pa, honest. Gussie and me earned it. Really. Ask Mr. Partridge at the Golf Club. I trained her to find golf balls and she's getting good at it. We found loads of good ones this morning and I got paid this much for them."

The two adults looked at the note on the table. Then they looked at each other. They realised what a difference this could make to them. His mother started to cry and rushed from the room and up the stairs. His father grabbed the boy and hugged him roughly.

"Well done, son! You and that mutt of yours could save our bacon. With that money, and the Dole, we might just get through this bad patch, after all. Good lad."

"But Da, why was me Ma cryin'?"

"Ah, son, that's one of the mysteries of life. Women is strange creatures. Sometimes they say one thing and mean another. Then they do something that means one thing one day and something else the next. There's no knowin' what's goin' on in their heads at all. But I know this, son, if you gets a good 'un, you're made for life. And, thank God, your Ma is one of the best."

"Is Gussie a good 'un too, Da?"

"Yes, son. Gussie is a good 'un, too."

❧ OUT OF THIS WORLD ❧

———————

HIS WIFE BROUGHT in a bowl of steaming soup, with freshly made brown bread, and put it on the table while he struggled with his shoelaces.

"There's your favourite wild mushroom soup, darling. Hurry now or you'll be late for your game."

"Ummm, that'll put 10 yards on my drives," he said, as he tasted it. "Where did you get the mushrooms?"

"From some children who called to the door."

Alan headed off to the Golf Club to meet his friends for a game. After nine holes, he and George Higgins were two down to Sam Wilson and Len Brownlow. The tenth hole is bordered by large sand dunes on the left, known locally as "Injun Country," and Alan hooked his tee shot deep into them. George sliced his tee shot into the rough on the right and their opponents were both up the middle. It looked as if they were going to go three down!

Alan trudged over to the foot of the dunes, picked a club out of his bag, left the cart on the fairway and climbed up and over the dunes. He told the others to play on so as not to waste time, and they continued to finish out the hole. Alan poked around in a desultory fashion for a few minutes, moving aside the long grass to the left and right as he looked for his ball. Having no luck, he decided to check one more time, just in case the ball had taken an unusual bounce. He slapped the grass aside and was amazed to hear a tiny voice.

"Be careful, Mister! That thing's dangerous."

Alan stared, unbelieving, at the bush. The voice came again, "Down here, noodle. We're not all as big as you!"

Alan looked around to see if his friends were playing a trick on him, but they were proceeding up the fairway toward the green and had no idea what was going on in the dunes. He stooped down to examine the bush more carefully. *Hearing voices in the dunes? What next?* he thought.

Gently parting the grass in a large clump, he stared in amazement at a tiny little man sitting on the ground beneath. Alan rubbed his eyes and looked again.

"Yes, I'm still here. You're not going off your head, either. You are looking at a genuine, true-blue, dyed-in-the-wool leprechaun. Didn't you ever hear of us?"

"Well, yes, I did but..."

"But you didn't believe what you heard."

"I, uh, well, not really, I suppose."

"You suppose! Now you'll be able to add to the legend. However, enough of this. My leg is caught in this rabbit trap and I've been here a week already. Be a good fellow and let me out."

Alan started to undo the cruel trap and then hesitated.

"Isn't there something about three wishes, in a situation like this?"

The little man scowled. "Well, alright, if you insist. What do you want?"

Alan thought rapidly. His friends were now on the green and would soon be moving on to the next tee.

"First of all, a really smooth putting stroke."

"No problem. Consider it done."

"Next, the ability to hit the ball, with any club, straight, left, or right at will."

"O.K., that's easy. The ball is yours to command from now on."

"Finally..." He hesitated. "Finally, I think I would like to be very good out of sand bunkers."

"Done! Now get me out of this infernal trap before I perish."

Alan completed the task of freeing the little man and he went on his way, limping badly but delighted to be free at last. Taking up the club he had laid on the ground while he undid the trap, Alan thoughtfully made his way back to his cart and up the fairway to his friends, who were a bit annoyed he had taken so long about looking for his ball.

"Come on, slowcoach," George said. "We haven't all day. What kept you?"

"Had to take a leak. Sorry for holding you up."

They grudgingly accepted his apology and proceeded to the next tee.

"You are now three down, lads," Sam said, "and, if I may say so, in deep trouble. Do you want a little side bet to recoup some of your losses?"

"No, thanks. One drubbing in a round is enough for me," said George. Alan concurred. His mind was not really on the game now. He was still thinking about his "experience" in the dunes. Had it really happened at all? He could not have been in there more than five minutes. Could he possibly have got through three wishes in that time? He laughed to himself and stood up to play his shot, having decided not to tell his companions what had transpired, just in case. The eleventh is a short par 3, so he hit a 7-iron and the ball flew straight and true at the pin. "Good shot, Alan. That leak must have taken a load off your mind!" laughed George.

His opponents smiled their congratulations, still confident that the money would be theirs at the end of the round.

The other three played their shots to the green but none of them "found the dance floor," so Alan had no difficulty in rolling in the putt for a birdie and a win. At the twelfth, his drive hit the bank on the right of the fairway and broke down to the left into the A-1 position. His 5-iron second shot took off like a jet from a runway and headed straight for the flag. It bounced 10 feet past it and spun back to within four feet. His companions were looking at him in awe.

"What God do you pray to, old boy?" George asked jokingly. "He's certainly pulling off a few miracles today!"

"Oh, just one of those things. I'll be back to normal soon."

"Not too soon, I hope," said a delighted George. "I want to get the money from these bandits first."

Alan found himself with the four-foot putt, a slight fall on it from left to right, for a win. He stood up to it, doing everything as he normally did, and made his new, smooth stroke at the ball. It rolled beautifully up to the hole and popped in, like a rabbit to a bolt hole. One down with six to play, a much improved position.

At the next hole, a short but tricky par 4, Alan's ball took off again on a direct line for the pin but a sudden gust of wind came and blew it off course into the quarry on the right. George caught a sand trap on the left and the other two were on the fairway. George, not renowned for his bunker play, left the ball behind in the sand at his first attempt and only barely managed to get it onto the green on his second. Alan lined up his pitch carefully and hit the ball sweetly along the chosen line. It hit the green and then kept rolling and rolling until it finally came to rest one inch short of the hole, dead on line.

"Great shot!" exclaimed George, relieved that his own effort could be overlooked in the match. Their opponents were so shocked by Alan's shot that they were hard pressed to halve the hole in three.

Still one down but now, with only five to play, the match was becoming very competitive. Once again Alan stood up on the fourteenth tee and unleashed a drive that, for him, was extraordinary in its direction and distance. An uneasy silence descended on their opponents, who could see their lead disintegrating before their eyes. This hole was a par 5 and another shot like that from Alan would mean he would be looking at a chip and putt for a birdie. He did marginally better, in fact, because his bullet of a second shot, from a perfect lie on the fairway, actually reached the front edge of the green, much to the amazement of all four golfers. Alan bit his lip to keep from shouting out in glee and telling them all what had happened in the dunes. It really seemed to be working! The little man had granted him his three wishes.

The putt, as they all now expected, rolled unerringly toward the hole and was only deflected from the true line by a worm cast about two feet short, leaving Alan with a tap-in for another birdie. Their opponents only secured a half by chipping into the hole.

One down with four to play. At the fifteenth, Alan's drive got a bad kick into the rough on the right of the fairway, leaving him with almost no way of getting on the green in two. Undaunted, when his turn came to play he opened his stance slightly, aimed up the left side of the fairway and hit the most magnificent controlled fade out of the rough. It was a shot that any top-class professional would have been proud of. By this time George was no more than an audience for Alan, rather than a partner. He was full of praise and applause for Alan's efforts, and the two opponents were reduced to going through the formalities of completing each hole. Alan was on a roll and there was no stopping him. This win made them level, with only three holes to play.

At the par-3 sixteenth hole, Alan, a bit overconfident, selected the wrong club for his tee shot and landed in a bunker.

"The man is human, after all," said one of his opponents, but Alan only smiled, remembering his third wish. The bunker shot he played was straight out of the instruction manual. It sailed over the pin, biting on the second bounce and spinning back, straight into the hole for another birdie. One up with two to play: a very nice position indeed.

The opposition was totally demoralised at this stage and they both topped their drives at the seventeenth hole, a par 4. George was chuckling so much that he had an air shot, missing the ball completely, and picked it up saying he would leave it to Alan to

administer the coup de grâce. This he duly did with a beautifully controlled fade drive down the left-hand side of the fairway, opening up the green on the right side where the pin was
positioned. He attacked the pin with a mid-iron that left him
with a 10-foot putt for another birdie, which he inevitably rolled
in with the confidence of a world champion. Match in the bag,
money in the pocket, let's hit the bar! Their opponents refused
the traditional "50% and a shot to save" bye on the last hole.
Enough was enough!

There was much talk in the bar (known in golfing circles as
the "nineteenth hole") among the four friends about the phe-
nomenal finish to Alan's round. He remained modestly quiet,
brushing it off as just one of those once-in-a-lifetime things. He
stuck to Ballygowan water and took his leave as soon as he de-
cently could.

As he sat in his car, his mind went back over the shots he had
played during those last eight holes. He wallowed in the satisfying feeling of total confidence that he had felt as he stood over
each of those shots. In his mind's eye he retraced the trajectory
of the drives and irons he had played with such professional com-
petence. He relished the feel of the putter and the roll of the ball
as it approached the hole. He replayed the bunker shot in slow
motion, with the sand spreading out like a fan around the ball as
he blasted it out, the first deceptive bounce that took it away
from the hole and the second crucial bounce that imparted the
spin through the ball to the grass on the green that caused it to
bite and return toward the hole, like a bird to its nest.

He was not aware of the only set of traffic lights in West
Clare as he sped through the village. The car shot straight

through and only the grace of God prevented a major catastrophe. He drove on, oblivious to his surroundings, until his consciousness was penetrated by the insistent sound of a siren. The police car passed him out and waved him down.

Fortunately for him, the court took a lenient view of his transgression. This was in light of the fact that he was found to have inadvertently consumed a hallucinogenic substance. His friends looked for their money back, but in vain.

His wife never bought wild mushrooms again.

ঙ OVER THE HILL ঙ

FIFTY IS A very big number for a man. There is no escaping it. It's a crossroads, a milestone and a millstone. The only way of avoiding it is by not getting there and, let's face it, in that case, you are decidedly worse off. The thoughtless young scoff at it, but, even as they scoff, they themselves are moving inexorably toward it. For years it seems to be miles away and then, all of a sudden, it's just around the corner. Harry Wheatfield was facing 50 on Friday.

There would be a party, of course, but that could be for any birthday. The only obvious manifestation that this was a special birthday was the bloody electric cart that his wife and children were jointly giving him as a present. The built-on seat was a bit over the top, he thought.

He had not as much hair as he used to have, and what was left was mostly gray. However, that could be covered with a hat and the guys never noticed the colour of your hair when they were paying up after losing a match on the golf course. The joints were stiffening, too, but not noticeably in public, and a little extra effort at fitness could keep that problem at bay for a while longer.

There was no way out of it that he could see, so he decided on a damage limitation exercise to alleviate the worst of the slagging. His short game was going to get the most unmerciful overhaul in the history of the game and there were going to be more sorry "boyos" in Lahinch this year, after losing money to him, than ever before. Dirty Harry was a-comin' to town!

Friday came and went and he smiled and said all the right things throughout the day. The next morning, he turned up on the first tee, none the worse for wear, with the brand-new, shining, white, electric pull-cart, complete with useful, but offensive, seat. Because he was expecting the slagging that occurred, he paid no attention and smiled benignly at everyone. His two regular playing partners were out for his blood in a big way, because they knew that if they failed to win the match, having given Harry such a hard time of it, he would surely make their lives miserable for the whole of the following week and, quite possibly, for several weeks after that.

The competition was intense all the way round and they arrived at the eighteenth tee all level in Stableford points. There was absolute silence as they played that final hole, each man striving desperately to avoid a fatal error, yet trying mightily to slip in one magic shot. They finished with three fives and remained all flat.

"That's great going for an auld fella," said Fred.

"Yes, indeed," chimed in Joe. "Have a good rest this afternoon, after all that hard work." They both laughed.

"Whaddaya mean, 'rest'?" said Harry sourly. "I'm not tired."

"Even at your age?"

This was a bit too much. Harry pursed his lips.

"O.K., hot shots. Double the bet and we'll keep going on a shootout basis, until the winner takes all. Put up, now, or shut up!"

"Ohhh, hit a raw nerve, have we?" laughed Joe. "O.K., I'm game. How about you, Fred?"

"I'm game, too. Let's go."

So they slipped into a gap between the late starters on the first tee and continued their game. A "shootout" meant that the player with the worst score at a hole dropped out of the game and the others continued until there is only one left.

Joe was the first to go, at the third, a tricky par 3 that requires a very accurate tee shot. He ended up in the "Vale of Tears" on the left and failed to get onto the green in two. His bogey was not good enough and Harry couldn't restrain a grin of satisfaction as Joe tossed his ball over the fence between the links and the amusement park in frustration.

The hill up to the fourth fairway got Fred. It tired him just enough for his concentration to slip. He pulled his second shot to the left, into the deep bunker in front of the green that lurks there for the unwary. Harry's little buggy practically pulled him up the steep slope and he had no difficulty making the green in two. Two putts and it was "game, set, and match."

Afterward, in the bar, Harry bought the winner's round of drinks and then sat silently, savouring the spoils of victory. He resisted the urge to slag, and kept his mouth shut. His two friends chatted to each other and to various friends as they passed in and out, but Harry remained aloof. Finally, Fred turned to him in exasperation.

"You're very quiet, Harry. Have you nothing to say for yourself?"

"Not really, Fred. You see, some guys do their talking in the bar, with their mouths. Some do it on the course, with their clubs. I've done a lot of talking today already, of the open-air variety. And you know what? It takes it out of you. Especially at *my* age."

✿ DANCING WITH DILY ✿

———

WE GET MANY types of visitors in Lahinch. Some are on a whistle-stop tour and pass through the place like scudding clouds across a sky, disappearing quickly in the distance, never to be seen or heard of again. Others, more sensibly, stay awhile and get to savour the whole ambience of the mecca of Irish Golf.

One such was J. Michael Rourke of Hilton Head in South Carolina, USA. Not only did J. Michael play a mean game of golf, he loved to have a little wager on it if at all possible. As luck would have it, this was also one of the many vices to which Bob Dickins succumbed, frequently.

One fine summer's evening, after the first tee had been cleared of all greenfee paying visitors and the caddies had been dispatched to their various abodes, Bob, who was a member of the club as well as an employee, a common enough situation in remote places like Lahinch, was resting quietly in a corner of the bar, enjoying a cool lager. He was sensible enough never to abuse the privilege he had of both membership and employment, and only used the bar in the clubhouse for light refreshment. When there was some serious drinking to be done, he had a favourite seat in the snug of the Golfer's Rest Lounge and Bar, halfway up Main Street in the village.

There happened to be some ladies' golf on the television and J. Michael, who had a tendency to chauvinism, could not restrain himself from commenting.

"Broads on TV golf!" he sneered. "It shouldn't be allowed. All they do is chat and hold up play."

The tip of Bob's nose started to tingle, as if a herpes blister was about to appear, although he had only half heard what the large American at the bar had said. The expression, "a nose for business," could have been coined especially for the proboscis attached to the ruddy face of Bob Dickins, so well did it pick out fruitful opportunities for profit. Bob drained his glass and sauntered up to the bar, now fully alert and with brain in top gear. He recalled what his spies—that is, the caddies he supervised—had told him about J. Michael. Big hitter, solid putter, adequate irons, but dodgy on short chips, capable of shooting in the mid-seventies during reasonable conditions.

"You're not casting aspersions on the fair sex, surely?" asked Bob, full of innocent charm, as he leaned his elbow on the bar conveniently near the American and signalled the barmaid for a refill.

"Why, not at all, my good man," said J. Michael patronisingly. "I just believe that golf is, essentially, a man's game and that the ladies, God bless 'em, are only dilettantes, dabbling at it."

"That would imply," said Bob, honing his hook before the strike, "that you believe that you could beat any lady in a flat match round this old links."

When the guns on the Western front stopped firing at the end of the Second World War, I'm told that there was a great silence. Some have compared that silence to the one that occurred after Bob's statement in the bar that evening. It hung in the air like a great cloud and no one breathed, swallowed, clinked ice, or crunched nuts until the response was forthcoming.

J. Michael was no fool. He knew that he either had to sh** or get off the pot. He assessed his current form carefully before replying, and, satisfied that all was in tip-top shape, smiled and said, "Yeah, I guess you could say that."

All the little bar noises resumed, but at a greatly reduced volume. Everyone wanted to hear what came next, although no one wanted to be obviously eavesdropping.

"I hope you'll forgive my temerity," said Bob, all polite sweetness, "but I beg to differ. I have 50 quid that says that Miss Dily would not be beaten by you in a flat match over 18 holes medal match play. She would be entitled to play off the ladies' tees, of course."

The markers had been carefully laid down.

J. Michael smiled. "Fifty quid? That's, like, pounds or punts, is it?"

"Indeed it is," said Bob, "or $79 at current exchange rates." It was Bob's business to know these things.

"Then $79 it is. Set it up. I'm here for the remainder of the week, staying at the Greenacres Guesthouse." He fished out his wallet and handed over 50 pounds to the head barman, whom

Bob had asked to hold the wager, to match Bob's money. It was ceremoniously sealed in an envelope and placed in the bar safe.

Bob shook hands with the big American and hightailed it out of the bar to the nearest phone, to lay his plans with Miss Dily Donworth, the Dame from Dooradoyle.

The designated day dawned damp and dreary, but the forecast was that it would brighten later, especially on the financial front. Eight in the morning was the starting time and, although there were few people in evidence, many eyes were watching. Bob stayed on duty in his Starter's Office, having assigned "The Phantom," the best caddie in Lahinch, to assist Dily on the way round. Some three hours later, the battling pair came to the eighteenth tee, with Dily one shot ahead. The form of competition specified by Bob called for every shot to be counted, unlike regular match play, where only holes are won and lost, regardless of the number of shots played overall. In addition, there would be no nineteenth-hole sudden-death playoff.

Bob emerged from his warm comfortable nest to observe the climactic moments from the back of the green. J. Michael blasted two woods onto the green and duly got his birdie. Dily was well short in two and pitched five yards past the pin for three. Her putt was always on the low side, but she had no trouble holing out for a five and a halved match in 75 gross.

J. Michael was magnanimous and shook Dily's hand mightily.

"Young lady, that was one of the finest rounds of golf I have ever seen played by a member of the fair sex. My congratulations. It is, if I may say so, entirely appropriate that no money should change hands after so sporting a game."

Dily simpered and bit her tongue.

The head barman appeared with the envelope and made to hand it to Bob.

"Just a minute, old son, ain't half of that mine?" queried J. Michael.

"It used to be but it's not any more," replied Bob. "The bet was for you to *beat* Miss Dily. You only equalled her score. You lose."

"Awww," said J. Michael, dumbstruck.

"Awww, indeed," said Bob, enjoying the moment. Turning to the small crowd, he continued, "Am I right or am I right?"

"Yes, indeed," the head barman concurred, "the terms of the wager clearly stated that you had to defeat Miss Dily in the match, sir. You definitely lose the wager."

J. Michael realised that he had made an amateurish mistake and took his medicine like a man.

"Let's go to the bar and have a little light refreshment," suggested Bob. They all agreed and trooped off the green, to a small round of applause from the gathered spectators.

Sitting around cool lagers 15 minutes later in the upstairs bar, they discussed the significant moments of the round.

"I can't help feeling that you pulled a fast one on me, Mr. Dickins," said J. Michael with a laugh, as they were finishing up their drinks and preparing to leave.

"Heaven forbid!" said Bob. "I would never do that to a visitor to our shores. I cannot allow you to leave in that frame of mind, spreading calumny all over the place. I'll tell you what. With Miss Dily's agreement, I'll offer you a return match. And this time, the winner takes all. Straight match play. Drawn match, no bet. Can't do fairer than that, now, can I?"

He looked at Dily. She smiled brightly and nodded. They all looked at J. Michael expectantly.

"Right," he said enthusiastically. "The only problem is that I'm scheduled to fly out of Shannon at noon the day after to-morrow. Can we fit it in before that?" They all looked at Dily.

"Ohhh, I'm a bit stuck for time," she said. "I'd have to take a day off from work. Could be a bit of a problem."

"Let me make it worth your while," said J. Michael grandly. "We'll increase the bet and, if you win, I'm sure Mr. Dickins will look after you. Whaddaya say?"

As Dily was already on a discreet 40% arrangement with Bob, this did not present any difficulty.

"What did you have in mind?" asked Bob.

"How about we double it?"

"Not worth the bother."

"You mean it's not enough?"

"Not really, when you consider that it has to be divided."

"What would be worth your while?"

"Would an extra nought onto the fifty be too rich for your blood?"

His pride would not let the American refuse. "Done."

Two days later, in the early morning, Dily blasted around the 14 holes of the Old Course that she needed to dispatch J. Michael Rourke by five and four, in three under par. He had no difficulty in catching his midday flight out of Shannon, a wiser, but poorer, man.

✧ A FISTFUL OF FEATHERS ✧

"WELL, JOCKSER, ARE you going to get your bird this year?" The loaded question was asked in the bar of Lahinch Golf Club a short while before Christmas.

"It was very embarrassing last year, you know. You were the only one of the gang not to get your turkey," his unkind friend continued. They all laughed. Jockser squirmed inside but put on a brave face in front of his buddies.

"Any day now, lads. Just you watch me."

He wasn't fooling anybody, not even himself. But he could not admit defeat while there were still a few turkey competitions left before Christmas. Especially after last year. Would he ever forget the kids' faces when he arrived home after the last competition and told them he hadn't gotten his bird? It was worse than when they found out that there was no Santa. The look of disappointment in their eyes was a killer. Well, not this year. Next weekend there would be two opportunities and he'd burst a gut if he had to, but he was going to get his bird!

He went three times to the driving range in Ennis after work in the following week and spent nearly a full hour over each bucket of golf balls, concentrating fiercely. He also practised his putting on the carpet at home. The children all gave him great encouragement, although he had to chase them from the room eventually because they were causing such a distraction. He found it particularly galling that his 10-year-old son could hit a target from a distance of five feet, 10 times out of 10, while he himself could rarely manage six. Wait until the kid grew up and found out how difficult it was. Then let him get 10 out of 10!

On the way home from the driving range, he usually called into The Golfer's Rest Bar and Lounge for a restorative pint. Belting golf balls was thirsty work. On one of these nights, as he was enjoying telling his friends how well he was swinging the club at the range, the barman badgered him into buying a raffle ticket out of the change from the round he had just bought. He put the ticket in his back pocket and got on with his story. Then he made his weary way home and dreamed of glories yet untold.

Saturday dawned bright and clear, but with a worrying breeze blowing from the southeast that was forecasted to increase. This lessened his chances considerably. The wind had a tendency to cause him to want to hit the ball harder, and this inevitably gave rise to mistakes. In the perverse game of golf, the harder you try, the less likely you are to succeed.

It's the same for everyone, he thought hopefully, and set off in his car. He had decided to play in the singles competition because he had a little difficulty in getting partners for the four-ball, due to his reputation as an "unlucky" golfer. His tendency to "freeze" over short putts probably didn't help, either. He figured that all the hotshots would have won their birds by now and their handicaps would have been decimated, theoretically, giving him a better chance. In any case, he told himself, he would rather get one on his own and not have to share the glory with another.

He struggled manfully along for 16 holes and then the strain became too much and he blasted two balls out-of-bounds onto the Liscannor Road on the seventeenth. Had he kept his head, even after that disaster, he might just have scraped in sixth or seventh, and still picked up a consolation bird, but he lacked even that much control. A topped drive and a shank on the eighteenth put paid to his score, and another chance was gone. Only one more competition to go.

A full hour putting on the carpet at home that night was his final preparation. He decided to try the four-ball on Sunday and made five phone calls before he came across one of his friends who couldn't think of a good enough excuse not to play with him the next morning. A few extra prayers before he jumped into bed and the rest was in the hands of the Lord.

He played "out of his skin" the next day and exceeded even his own expectations. He made no serious errors and 19 times out of 20 he would have had a winning score. But it takes two to make a good four-ball score and his partner had a ferocious hangover and was useless on the day. They missed a bird by one point. He was gutted.

For consolation, he called into The Golfer's Rest on the way home, even though it was Sunday and he had an understanding with his wife that the pub was out-of-bounds on the day of rest.

The barman hailed him. "Congratulations, auld son! Yer ticket came up last night. I have your prize out here in the back."

He disappeared for a minute and then plonked it on the table in front of Jockser. Other customers smiled their good wishes and clapped him on the back. He beamed at everyone and bought a round of drinks that he could ill afford, for Christmas was an expensive time with kids. Finishing up his own drink, he headed off home with a light heart.

The kids saw him coming from the front window and charged out to greet him, dying to know had he "got the bird." All the neighbours could hear the racket, he was pleased to note, and he took a little longer to make the trip, with the prize, from the car to his front door than was really necessary. He marched into the kitchen, where his wife was getting the Sunday lunch ready, and laid it gently on the table.

"One 20-pound, free-range, hen turkey for the Christmas dinner, as promised," he said, preening. The kids all cheered. "Let's eat it today," they yelled in their excitement.

"Away with you all, now," said his wife, smiling. "You'll have to wait for the twenty-fifth, just like Santa."

"How did you win, Da?" they asked in awe. "Did you tear the place apart?"

"Ah, now, children, modesty forbids. I can't be boring your mother with a blow-by-blow account of the full 18 holes. Let's just say that I had a bit of luck."

His wife herded the kids out of the kitchen and turned to him.

"I suppose you know," she teased him gently, "that you could have bought two turkeys, the ham and a piece of Dan Olden's best spiced beef with the money you spent trying to win that auld bird?"

"Ah, yes, dear," he replied. "But they'd never taste as good."

♣ A Christmas Story ♣

Season of goodwill, how are ya? Season of cold warfare, more likely. It was so refined, so sophisticated, so bloodless, that you would hardly know it was going on at all. But it was, and there were fatalities and walking wounded. I am referring, of course, to the rivalry between the minimalist and traditionalist factions of the Ladies' Branch of Lahinch Golf Club with regard to the Christmas tree decorations.

I cannot understand how or why it broke out in such epic proportions that year. I have known years when there was almost total unanimity on the subject. Hordes of jolly lady golfers dancing and prancing around the tree, exchanging gossip and tearing people apart with reckless but harmonious abandon.

I think, on reflection, that the first mistake was the Captain's. Generally speaking, I am a great supporter of the Captain of the Club for about 11 months of the year. But, come December, I have to take a more jaundiced view of the man. On this occasion, he definitely got it wrong when he asked the chairperson of the Ladies' House Committee to take charge of the decorating. She was a minimalist. The proper protocol would have been to solicit—in the nicest possible way, of course—the Lady Captain herself, to take on the job. She was a traditionalist, so one could see the potential for conflict immediately. The situation was not irretrievable even at that stage, if the good chairperson had had the diplomacy to seek the Lady Captain's blessing for the project, just at a time of the year when she might be in need of some slight reassurance that she was still revered and respected as the principal lady golfer in the Club, instead of the lame duck that reality dictated. But no, it was not to be. The chairperson launched in with two left feet and before anyone knew what was going on she had spent 300 pounds on some fancy new decorations from Todds in Limerick, which she proceeded to apply to the two trees in the clubhouse—one in the reception hall and the other upstairs in the bar.

The words were not recorded at the next Ladies' Committee meeting but my sources tell me that the final result was referred to scathingly as "a seminaked tree without even the saving grace of a set of coloured lights." The good chairperson had used a set of plain lights that blinked irritatingly every few seconds and were held responsible for at least one Christmas celebrant in the bar slipping senseless from his stool, rather in the manner of some helicopter pilots who were dazzled by searchlights from below that reached them through the whirling blades of other machines in the sky.

Initially, nothing was said overtly. Additional decorations simply appeared mysteriously on the trees. It was obvious even

to Bob Dickins that the new additions were quite out of keeping with the original decor. His remark that "it looked like a
blind man with a hangover had done the job" was bandied about
in the village with great glee. At least some people were getting
some Christmas cheer out of the situation!

Things took a more serious turn when the offending additions began to disappear, equally mysteriously. Even the eagle-
eyed Bob could not ascertain who exactly the culprit was from
his vantage point across the first tee, even though the dogs in
the street knew who the instigators must have been. Nothing
was ever proved, however.

The scene turned nastier still when certain ladies took their
names off certain time sheets for no apparent reason, for normally these girls turned up for their turkey competitions in the
autumn, come hell or high water, and their dedication to the pur-
suit of the bird was the envy of even some of the menfolk. The
only possible explanation was that someone else on the particular line of the time sheet had contrary views on the decorations.

After the Lady Captain's Dinner, however, Monsignor
O'Flaherty himself, the president of the Club, became concerned
when he learned that the tables had split into the two camps of
pro and con and that some bread rolls had been exchanged
through the air between the rival factions. And that was before
the wine had been served! The slagging that went on after inhi-
bitions had been loosened up by the demon drink were such that
my normally reliable and loquacious sources would admit to no
more than that things "got a wee bit out of hand."

This turned out to be a slight understatement, as other
sources available to a resourceful Secretary/Manager (i.e., the

catering staff) reported that one particularly vociferous supporter of the minimalist school had the dessert that she had prepared and brought to the festivities herself, as was the custom
among the ladies, dumped in her lap by someone of the opposite persuasion, with the suggestion that the following year she
should get her contribution from Dunnes Stores in Ennis, as it
was bound to be more palatable. Shocking stuff!

The names of the perpetrators shall never pass my lips, of
course. Suffice it to say that several of the ladies' teams would
be bereft of some of their best players should the sordid details
ever become public knowledge.

"Fr. Malachy, what can be done to resolve this unseemly
contretemps?" asked the Monsignor, with a worried look on his
face. "It's bringing the Club into disrepute!"

"Well, Monsignor, that's a difficult one. 'Tis a brave man
indeed that would insert himself in the middle of that lot."

The Parish Priest noted the young curate's perspicacity.

"Perhaps you could enquire among your friends, as discreetly
as possible, what might be done to resolve the matter?"

"Indeed I will, Monsignor. With the utmost discretion."

It was Dr. Joe Moore, practical man that he was, who came
up with the solution. It did verge on the drastic and required
several men of stout heart and strong hand to carry it off. Or,
rather, carry them off. For that was what they did. With my
own connivance (for someone had to turn off the alarm system
when they came in the dead of night), they whipped off the decorations, bundled the trees into two waiting vans drawn up to the
back of the clubhouse and spirited them off to two poor but
deserving families. One was in Miltown Malbay and the other

in Lisdoonvarna. They had been selected for their location out of potential harm's way.

One family got the entire collection of "modern" decorations, which made the one tree look quite handsome and the other got several boxes of assorted baubles assembled over the years by the Club which looked absolutely fabulous to them when lit up with an old set of multicoloured lights discovered at the bottom of a box.

Honour was satisfied on both sides, as, technically, no one had surrendered. The incoming Captain, however, was taken aside by the Monsignor, who was going forward again as president, and warned to get in an independent male interior decorator, preferably from outside the county, to do the tree decorating the following year, and to hell with the expense.

❧ THE BOSNIAN BOMBSHELL ☙

———

"HURRY, TIM, I don't want to keep the poor girl waiting at Limerick Junction."

Marie Twomey fussed about. Sergeant Tim Twomey went to bring the car around from the side of the Garda Station to the front door so that his wife and eldest daughter, Grainne, could get in, and then they set off at a cracking pace for Limerick Junction railway station, some 15 minutes or so beyond Limerick City.

"What'll she be like, Mam?" asked Grainne, full of 15-year-old curiosity.

"Well, love, the people at the agency were a bit vague. All I know, as I've told you several times before, is that she is about 20 years old, dark-haired, very thin and worn out from the terrible time they had in that God-forsaken country, and she's in dire need of some peace and quiet, lots of rest, good food, and plenty of TLC."

"What's TLC, Mam?"

"Tender Loving Care, pet, and, thanks be to the Good Lord, we have lots of that to spare in our family, so we are going to share it with this unfortunate child."

"But she's not a child, Mam, she's 20."

"To adults, pet, she's still a child."

They were in good time for the arrival of the midday train from Dublin, and their hearts went out to the bedraggled, tousle-haired bag of bones carrying a battered old cardboard suitcase that emerged from the train under the guidance of a kindly conductor, who had been asked to keep an eye on the Bosnian refugee.

"Zeelya Izabeghavitch?" asked Marie, when she saw them approaching. The bewildered girl nodded and Marie Twomey took the suitcase gently from her and gave it to Tim to carry. Then she wrapped her in a mighty embrace and hustled her toward the waiting car. Passing through Limerick, an old banger backfired and the terrified girl threw herself onto the floor of the moving vehicle and screamed.

"Hush, hush, child," said Marie, "that's nothing at all. Just some old car having trouble with its engine."

When she had been seated properly once again she sheepishly said her first words.

"I shorry. Big bang in Sarajevo mean bik trooble." Her thick Slavic accent was difficult to understand at first.

"I know, pet," said Marie, holding her close, "but you don't have to worry now. Where we're going there is no big trouble. Take it easy while we make our way home. Tim, slow down! Where do you think you are? Mondello Park?"

The Sergeant obediently eased off the accelerator and the quieted girl gazed at the passing countryside through big dark eyes. Zeelya Izabeghavitch was emerging from the hell that was Sarajevo to the paradise that was Lahinch.

Shortly after they had arrived home and were having a refreshing cup of tea in the Twomey kitchen, neighbours began to arrive with little treats for the traveller and, of course, to satisfy their natural curiosity about this stranger in their midst. The still-frightened girl gave each visitor a wan smile as they entered, left their welcoming gift, and were quickly ushered out again by the woman of the house.

When Marie saw that the girl was getting tired, she shooed everyone out of the way and hustled her upstairs, where she ran her a hot bath and gave her some warm fluffy towels from the airing cupboard. She couldn't help noticing, as the girl climbed out of her old rags, how well developed she was as a young woman, despite a degree of emaciation from the traumatic times she had been through.

Marie left out new cotton pyjamas for her and realised that she would only barely fit into them, as she had only estimated her size and had, for some reason, expected a small person, rather than this fully grown but underfed young adult. Not to worry. She packed her off to bed and threatened dire consequences to anyone, bar none, who did anything to wake the sleeping refugee upstairs.

The girl slept for the rest of the afternoon and right through the night. She awoke midmorning the next day to go to the bathroom and afterward packed away a hearty Irish breakfast-in-bed before hitting the pillows for another eight hours' sleep, followed by supper and another full night's rest.

"The poor child," Marie said to her husband. "She has months of deprivation to make up for, God love her."

"And no better woman to get her back on her feet," said Tim, giving Marie a big hug.

"It's the least we could do. Hasn't the Lord been good to us, with four fine children, a roof over our heads, a steady income, and plenty of food on the table? Why wouldn't we give her a helping hand?"

The recuperation continued over the next two weeks, under Marie's careful supervision and excellent cooking. Dr. Angela was called in to check her over. She prescribed plenty of rest, food, milk, sleep and fresh air, and exercise as soon as she felt able for it.

"What age is she?" the doctor asked Marie after her examination.

"I understand she's 20."

"Well, she'll be a fine looking girl when she's fully recovered. And she's got a lovely face, too, offset by those great dark eyes. I wouldn't be surprised if there are soon a few broken hearts among the young bloods of Lahinch." Both women laughed.

On the Thursday of the third week of her stay, Tim was cleaning his clubs when Zeelya, now fully recovered after Mrs. Twomey's careful nurturing, walked unexpectedly in on him.

"Do you torture people in this police station?" she asked, fingering the strange implements.

"Not at all, girlie. They're not for torturing people. At least not in the physical sense," he laughed. "They are golf clubs, for playing a game."

He took one out to show her. Gingerly, she took it in her hand and held it like a sword.

"How you play wiv dis?" she asked, waving it about, as if fending off an attacker.

Tim took it back from her and, putting a ball down on the carpet, held the club by the grip and hit the ball gently across the room and out into the hallway.

"There," he said. "That's what we do with it. We hit a little white ball around a big field into many little holes and whoever does it in the least number of shots is the winner."

"Some crazy game!" she offered.

"I'll tell you what, Zeelya," said Tim, in a moment of magnanimous madness, "I'll bring you out with me to see the game being played this afternoon. How's that?"

"HoKay," she said before going on her way.

Tim thought no more of it until he was loading the car with his gear after lunch. She emerged from the house wearing white shorts that were too short and a tank top that was too tight. Both garments failed to meet at any point, thus revealing a large expanse of Bosnian bellybutton and a cleavage that could go on the stage. He beat a hasty retreat into the house to find his wife.

"I can't take her out looking like that," he said. "It's a golf game, not a beach party. What will people say?"

"Never mind what people will say. You're doing your bit for this poor child refugee from Bosnia. Go on with you and don't be annoying me," said Marie, secretly amused at his discomfiture.

Tim huffed and puffed a bit as he beat an undignified retreat and it was with some misgivings that he got into the car with the young lady. He couldn't understand how his wife could not see the problem. But then again, maybe she did. Perhaps the stuffed shirts at the Golf Club needed a bit of a shake-up!

On the way down to the club, which was not more than a couple of hundred yards away, Tim explained briefly what was expected of her as a caddie. As she sauntered over toward the right-hand side of the first tee, pulling Tim's pull-cart behind her, she attracted many admiring glances—and it wasn't for her bag-pulling technique either. Dr. Joe, Tom Rourke, and Father Malachy made up the rest of the four-ball. Tom tapped Tim on the shoulder.

"Is this some kind of secret weapon you've brought out to disable the opposition?"

"No," snapped Tim, "I'm only showing her the ropes."

"Wouldn't mind showing her the ropes myself," said Tom, walking away smiling.

Fully aware of the attention she was attracting, Zeelya continued over to the tee and, seeing the sign over Bob Dickins's window, went across to it. She put her elbows on the ledge and, leaning through the open window, she gave the people on the tee the opportunity to view the vast expanse of her posterior while she gave Bob such an eyeful that, for one of the few occasions in his life, he regretted his commitment to bachelorhood.

"Vould you be my master, too, as I am caddie now?" she asked.

Bob Dickins was stuck for a reply, a most unusual occurrence, as his eyes were riveted on the twin Mount Igmans leaning into his office. He shuffled some papers importantly and retreated into the loo, not to be seen for the rest of the day, surrendering his perch at the window to his second-in-command.

The four players eventually hit off and, as they walked up the fairway, Zeelya asked, "Vhy everybody take two, three shots to hit leetle ball?"

"The first one or two are practice shots, dear," explained Tim.

As they each went off to play their second shots from various parts of the course, she observed all the goings-on around her. Standing on the left of the first green, where Tim had instructed her to remain, she demanded to know, "Vhy you not all hit up the meeddle? It much shorter and have no big holes filled with sand."

"That, indeed, is the aspiration of every golfer, my dear," explained Father Malachy kindly, "but it is not given to all of us to be so accurate."

"Maybe if you practise more, you hit leetle ball straight," she suggested helpfully, shrugging her shoulders, which had the effect of shaking several other wobbly parts of her ample body. The four men looked away.

On the first green, they had between them two three-putts, a four-putt, and only one orthodox two-putt.

"I teenk, perhaps, maybe bigger leetle hole be good idea." This eminently sensible suggestion was met with a stony silence.

After observing the rituals on the second tee, she enquired, "Vhy you need all those clubs? In my country ve share very much things."

"It's the rules, you see. We are not allowed."

"Crazy rules," was her comment.

On the second hole, a par 5, Dr. Joe found a fairway bunker off the tee with his drive and, after his third shot, went into another bunker beside the green, from which he took three more shots to get out.

"Vhy bik man play in sand like that?" Zeelya asked in wonderment.

"It's a bit more difficult to hit the ball out of the sand," explained the good Father, although his patience was being stretched a bit by now.

They all made pars at the short third hole and this cheered them up a bit. They moved on to the fourth, and when they reached the green, Tim directed Zeelya to go to the next tee, off on the left, and wait for them. This she dutifully did and, observing what was going on down on the beach, she innocently did likewise. When Tim came over to the tee, after the hole was completed, he was horrified to see that she had stripped off her tank top, unclasped her recently acquired Wonderbra, and was lying face down taking the sun on her back and the rather substantial bits of bosom that were peeking out from under her chest.

"Jasus, Zeelya, get yer clothes on quick, before Father Malachy sees ye. What do you think you are doing? This isn't the beach!"

Tim tried desperately to form a barrier between the others and the half-naked girl, as she gave him an eyeful that kept him distracted for the next three shots while she struggled to cover herself up again.

When they had all hit off the fifth tee and just Tim and herself were left behind, cleaning Tim's driver and looking for the bottle of cold orange in the bag, she asked plaintively, "Vhy dis beach and dat not beach?" pointing to a spot five yards away from the tee, just outside the wire boundary.

"It's the rules," said Tim in exasperation.

"Crazy rules," she said under her breath.

As she sat on the wall behind the green at the Klondyke, she took another sip of the cold orange from the bag. She dribbled some down her front and a nearby wasp, as any self-respecting wasp would, made a beeline for the tasty trickle. She jumped up and, screaming, tried to whoosh the offending black-and-amber intruder out of the curvaceous crevice, but to no avail. In desperation, she gripped the lower edge of both tank top and bra at the front and pulled them over her head, thus releasing the trapped intruder but, in the process, exposing her glorious bosom to all and sundry. Tom O'Rourke claimed afterward that he had never lifted his head so quickly in his life before, with such beneficial effects.

A tour bus driver who had the good fortune to be passing along the public road just at that moment also suffered a major distraction. In his excitement, he nearly used his bus to demolish the back end of the fifth green. Fortunately, he pulled the bus off the ditch in time and sustained only minor damage to the front left wing of the vehicle. The Japanese tour group travelling in the back of the bus was bemused by the dark-haired young lady dancing topless on the green with four middle-aged men waving golf hats and handkerchiefs about her in a vain attempt to cover up her nakedness. They took loads of photos with their ever-ready cameras and brought home some very interesting mementoes of their visit to the West of Ireland.

With God's dear little winged creature off in the fresh air, order was restored to the fifth green, with Wonderbra and tank top safely in place and decorum stalking the links once again. But Tim Twomey had had enough. Taking Zeelya by the hand, he walked her over to the road and, pointing south to where the Garda Station could be seen about a mile away, he suggested, with the air of a man who would not be contradicted, that she was tired and that perhaps she had better make her way slowly homeward, taking care of the traffic on the narrow road, and on the strict understanding that she keep her clothing on at all costs. His mind boggled as to how he was going to explain all this to his good wife when he got home. Zeelya sauntered off down the road, creating havoc on both sides of the ditch as she went.

"Well," said Father Malachy in an effort to lighten the atmosphere, "Monsignor O'Flaherty should hear some very interesting stories in Confession this month." They all laughed, but none of them broke 90 on their own cards for the round and it was some days before their natural equanimity was restored.

In the pubs throughout the village that night, the tales of Zeelya's doings went the rounds, and the size of her mammary glands grew with each telling and the number of garments that the girl had removed in what was, after all, a genuine emergency, multiplied to the point where the dance of the seven veils paled in comparison. The womenfolk had mixed feelings about it. Some praised her for having the courage to do what was necessary. Others considered that her carry-on was inexcusable.

Several busloads of Japanese tourists could be observed over the next week cruising up and down Millionaire's Row, as the Liscannor Road was known locally, apparently going nowhere but peering intently out the windows as the bus passed by the fifth green. Bob Dickins had numerous nightmares involving wasps.

Mrs. Twomey made sure that Zeelya was well covered up every time she went out in public thereafter. Slowly the village returned to normal. It remained that way until the dinner after the Captain's Prize, to which Mrs. Twomey, God bless her innocence, had insisted that Zeelya be taken. Sergeant Tim tried valiantly to resist, but to no avail. He just could not find the right words to explain to his devoted, God-fearing wife that the girl was a sex bomb waiting to go off and that Lahinch just was not ready for her, and was unlikely to be for another two decades at least.

Nobody remembers the winner of the Captain's Prize that year. The winning score was forgotten before the presentation was over. The Captain himself played only a minor role. Zeelya was the star that day.

Mrs. Twomey had lent her a little black number, from her younger days, for the occasion. With a bit of skilled needlework, a nip here, a tuck there, and the removal of surplus material in one strategic area, Zeelya altered the demure little black number that the nuns had approved of when first purchased and transformed it into a sheath of dynamite that was to cause an explosion in the village, the reverberations from which would ring around the whole County of Clare for years to come.

The full effect of the combination of the alterations and Zeelya's fuller figure was not revealed until it was too late, for she appeared from her room only at the last minute and had taken the precaution of tying a shawl across her shoulders. Upstairs in the bar at the club, she likewise kept the shawl in place while having a drink before the dinner, but, when she stood up to go to the dining room and let the shawl slip to the floor, she caused a sensation. Nearly every red-blooded male in the room rushed to escort her to her table. At least 10 single young men paraded up to her during the meal to book a dance for later and the only reason the number wasn't greater was that the married men were held firmly in place by their panicking spouses.

At the dance afterward, she led the conga around the club-house, blithely unaware of the fights going on behind her amongst the men who were vying with each other to get their hands around her swaying hips. She gave an exhibition of her new silk underwear, what there was of it, in the course of a rock 'n' roll number that caused Monsignor O'Flaherty to wish that the ban on that kind of music would be brought back. All of the men, married or unmarried, with whom she danced throughout the night had the course of their lives changed forever.

There is still debate in the village as to whether the traditional auction at the end of the evening was a good or a bad thing. True, the local charities that benefited from it never had such a large donation in the history of the club. But afterward there were many soreheads and several worried bank managers, and a few rocky marriages nearly tipped over into the abyss.

The custom was for the single girls attending the dinner to offer themselves for auction for the last dance of the evening, the proceeds going to various worthy causes. This gave the local swains an opportunity to nail their colours to the mast and a few unlucky lovers/boyfriends/fathers the difficult, if not impossible, task of explaining to their wallflowers just why they were unable to match some of the exorbitant bids made for their more fortunate sisters.

The auctioneer for the evening, a cute Kerry hoor, insisted on starting the auction with Zeelya, knowing full well that she was likely to attract a good price and that the bidders for the remaining girls would be honour-bound to bid in similar terms. Little did he know that she would attract a bid three times higher than the record achieved before (and that had been by an American millionaire for his overweight, pimply daughter who was eating her way around Europe).

Zeelya helped matters along hugely by accosting each bidder in turn and assuring him with kisses and hugs and much body contact that whatever price he paid would be only a quarter of the value he would get from her in the course of the last dance. One young man offered to sell his much-prized, hand-restored Harley-Davidson motorbike, but he was spared this painful sacrifice when the bidding for Zeelya far outstripped the paltry sum he had thus raised. Another offered a recently acquired set of very expensive golf clubs and, when the sum offered for the clubs was found to be inadequate to purchase the favours of the lovely Zeelya, he had to be restrained from throwing himself out of the window onto the concrete path below.

Zeelya, dissatisfied with the final bid for her favours, insisted on clearing the dance floor in front of the auctioneer's stand and, to a lively modern number, performed a Balkan fandango that left no one in any doubt about the rich treasures he would be bidding for. When the bidding started up again after her exhibition dance, there were tears in the eyes of many of the males in the company, some of whom had been whipped up into a positive frenzy and had to be spoken to by the good Monsignor. The ladies looked on in grim-faced silence.

Three more bids were received before the record-breaker from an old bachelor from Doolin who had decided to mortgage the farm if necessary to dance with this divine virago, even if it was the last thing he did on God's earth. There were howls of anguish from the younger men whose bids had failed when the winner was revealed. He tottered up to the podium to claim his prize and was grabbed by the still effervescing Zeelya, who kissed him full on the lips and nearly squeezed the life out of him with the hug that accompanied it. When the poor man fainted from lack of oxygen and the excitement of it all, the young swains demanded that she be put up for auction again, but Monsignor O'Flaherty was having none of it. He insisted that the auctioneer proceed to the next young lady, who was already in tears, anticipating that the bids for her would go nowhere near the record bid for Zeelya. She wasn't disappointed. She snuffled her way to her successful suitor and swore that she would never speak to him as long as she lived after making such a paltry bid for her favours, and told him in no uncertain terms that he could abandon any plans that he had for taking her home in his beat-up old jalopy afterward.

It continued thus until all the remaining girls were "sold." Two engagements were called off shortly after that dance and three "near certainties" suffered fatal consequences. The man from Doolin never fully recovered from his encounter with Zeelya and died some months later, the doctors pondering whether it was from a broken heart or a ruptured spleen. While he was receiving first aid out on the landing where there was still some fresh air, Zeelya grabbed Fr. Malachy and said, "Dance vith me, leetle man, I luf your boody."

Fr. Malachy was mortified. Taking a quick look round to establish the whereabouts of Monsignor O'Flaherty and seeing that he was out of harm's way on the landing saying prayers over the prostrate farmer, he decided to enter into the spirit of the occasion and did not refuse, much to the chagrin of the laymen in the room. The next five minutes truly shook his vocation to its foundations. Fair dues to the man, he withstood the test and emerged a better priest for it afterward. He did, however, change his opinion about married clergy and contraception, from that day on.

At the end of the dance, Zeelya kissed most of the men in the room and faithfully promised to save each and every one of them a dance at the next hooley, which was planned for the local Sports and Community Centre in a week's time. This had a twofold effect on the village of Lahinch and the surrounding district that night. A goodly number of bedroom doors were slammed shut in the faces of bewildered menfolk and spare rooms that had not already been rented out were brought into emergency use. Those without spare bedrooms spent the remainder of the night in various strange but universally uncomfortable locations. The remainder had a rollicking good time with their more understanding spouses or girlfriends.

Zeelya never did make it to the next hooley in the Sports and Community Centre. She received a phone call the very next day from the Embassy in London informing her that her family had been located in a recently liberated refugee camp in northern Bosnia, and she set off at once to join them.

The whole village was stunned, locals and visitors alike, half with relief and the other half with a great sense of loss. Everyone realised that a powerful force had passed through their lives, one that men fought wars over, undertook great adventures for and occasionally died for. It was bigger than home, family, country and, they realised with some dismay, bigger even than golf itself!

✥ Lessons ✥

"Aw, Daaaad, you promised!"

The doleful sound of a disappointed daughter.

"But sweetie, I'm playing golf on Saturday with your Steve. I won't have time to give you a driving lesson. I'll be giving *him* one instead!" Lorna's father guffawed.

"Dad, you're not to win any more money off Steve. He's always in a bad humour afterward and takes it out on me. Anyway, you should be ashamed of yourself for even playing him for money. He has only been at that silly game for three years. You've been playing since olden times. Anyway, your game is not until 11 o'clock."

"Now, now, young lady. None of your lip or you'll be getting no driving lesson from me."

"Does that mean you'll give me one on Saturday after all?" gushed Lorna, completely ignoring what her father had actually said. She rushed over to him and planted a big mushy kiss on his cheek, in typical only-daughter fashion, and, before he could say anything more, she disappeared into the kitchen, calling out to her mother that she had a driving lesson lined up with her Dad for 9:30 the following Saturday morning, thus making it impossible for the poor man to get out of the situation without incurring the wrath of the first lady in his life, who just happened to dote on the second lady in his life.

Lorna went out later that evening to tell her long-standing boyfriend, Steve, the good news. She chided him for thinking her father would not have obliged her, the only daughter in the family and well known as the apple of his eye.

"Would you like another pint before we go?" asked Lorna, reaching for her purse.

"No thank you, love, I've had enough. Too much of this stuff keeps me awake at night. I want to be fit and fresh for the game tomorrow. Let's go."

Lorna went happily to sleep later that night. She dreamed of big cars and incredible hulks of the male species being awestruck with her style and speed on the narrow roads of West Clare.

Willy Roberts had to get up earlier than intended that Saturday morning because the time he had earmarked for a lie-in had been purloined by his darling daughter for her driving lesson.

Imagine! he thought to himself in wonder. *Little Lorna old enough to have driving lessons! How time flies! It seems like only last week I was bouncing a ball of fat and nappies on my knee, and here she is now, nearly all grown up.*

After breakfast he called to his daughter to come for the lesson, but she was still fussing in front of the mirror in her bedroom, putting on her makeup.

"Lorna, pet, will you hurry on. I'm playing golf at eleven."

"I have to put on my face, Dad. Suppose I meet someone!"

"Who are you expecting to meet on the back roads of West Clare at this ungodly hour of a Saturday morning?" her father asked. "Would you get a bit of sense, girlie. And even if you did meet Roger Moore, you'd be whizzing along so fast he wouldn't have time to appreciate your dazzling beauty. Now, I'm off. Are you coming or not?" said Willy as he marched out to the car, half annoyed and half bemused with his only daughter, as usual.

"Mum, who on earth is Roger Moore?"

"A hero from your father's past, darling. Now, be a good girl and hurry up. You don't want to upset your father when he is putting himself out for you. It'll take more than one lesson to get you driving, so don't mess up now."

"Yes, Mum," said Lorna resignedly, knowing her mother was right but wanting desperately to look her best for her very first driving lesson. Five minutes later she finally plonked into the passenger seat of the car beside her gently fuming father.

"Well, Dad, what are you waiting for? Drive on!"

Willy stalled the engine in frustration and his only daughter burst out laughing, as did his wife who was discreetly watching the proceedings from an upstairs window.

He drove out beyond Ennistymon toward the north, and when he came to a quiet part of the road he stopped and explained in simple terms how the various parts of the car interacted to make it go forward, backward, faster, and slower. After assuring him that she understood all these minor details perfectly, Lorna couldn't wait to get into the driver's seat to take control.

She raced the engine until it whined in agony, grated the gears painfully into first, without the benefit of a fully engaged clutch, took her foot off the accelerator and the clutch at the same time and had her head nearly rocked off her neck when the car jumped forward erratically several times, finally dying in its tracks. She let out a little scream.

"Easy, isn't it?" asked her slightly cynical father, who was rather enjoying her discomfiture.

They tried again, several times in fact, and eventually she got the car going forward in second gear. The word "forward" is used loosely, for there was a degree of left ditch, right ditch about her progress that should not be overlooked.

"Try not to look at the floor when you are changing gears, pet. Keep your eye on the road ahead."

"But I can't see what I'm doing."

"You'll get used to it. Just *feel* where the correct position is. Don't try to *see* it."

"Yes, Dad."

"Increase the speed a bit now, take your foot off the accelerator, put in the clutch, and put her in third gear."

Lorna followed the instructions, but could not find the slot for third gear and couldn't resist looking down.

"MIND THE DITCH," roared Willy, grabbing the wheel and yanking the car back onto the road. Lorna squealed. The car stalled and they had to start the routine all over again.

Some miles up the road, Willy decided that it was time they returned home, so he asked Lorna to pull into a tourist lay-by.

"Now, put it into reverse, let the clutch out very slowly, turn the steering wheel well to the left, and ease the car slowly backward."

Lorna tried to follow these instructions, but forgot to straighten out the steering wheel, so the car proceeded in a semi-circle and was heading for a sturdy West of Ireland stonewall.

"HIT THE BRAKE."

Fortunately for all concerned, the poor girl managed to do that just in time, thus avoiding a very expensive end to her lesson. Willy's heart was racing.

"Now, love, put the hand brake on because the car is on a slight incline. Clutch in, first gear, gentle acceleration and ease the clutch out, then release the hand brake and off we go."

She got as far as "release the hand brake" before her brain overloaded and she short-circuited. The car shuddered to a halt.

"O.K., O.K., pet. We'll try that again and I'll do the hand brake bit this time. Ready?"

This time they got away and chugged back toward Ennistymon.

"Dad, is there something wrong with this car, or are they all so difficult to drive?"

"Don't turn your head when you are talking to the passenger, pet. The driver must watch the road ahead at all times."

"Yes, Dad. But are all cars so difficult to drive?"

He hesitated mentioning cars with automatic transmissions in case she instituted a campaign to get one. He fudged the issue, a tactic he frequently employed when dealing with his darling daughter.

"You'll get used to it, love, honestly. After a few more lessons you won't even know you're changing gears, it will come so naturally to you."

"I'll never get used to this..."

"MIND THAT BUS!"

The Japanese tour bus narrowly missed them and Willy decided he had had enough. He insisted on reclaiming the driver's seat and they headed for home. Lorna flounced out of the car when they arrived at the house and complained bitterly to her mother about the difficulties she had experienced.

"You never really know a man until he gives you a driving lesson!" she proclaimed profoundly.

"Wait until you get married, darling," replied her mother sagely.

Willy beat a hasty retreat, as he realised that he was in a no-win situation. He made his way to the Golf Club for his game as quickly and quietly as he could. He met one of his playing partners on the first tee.

"Well, young Steve, how much do you want to lose today?"

"Let's make it a bit more interesting today. How about 20?"

"Twenty, indeed. You must be feeling lucky! O.K., 20 quid it is. On the card?"

"On the card it is," said Steve.

The third member of their three-ball arrived and they set off in the Stableford singles competition. Steve concentrated very hard over the first five holes and it paid off. He was only two over par and had 12 points on the card, thanks in part to his 14 handicap.

Willy, however, was struggling. His mind was still in turmoil after the near misses of the driving lesson and, consequently, was not entirely on his game. He could only manage seven points for the same holes—a five-point gap. He struggled manfully for the rest of the first nine but finished up with only 15 points. Steve had 21.

Willy managed to close the gap to three points by the time they came to the seventeenth tee. Just as he was about to drive off, one of those huge Japanese touring buses roared by, stirring up the turmoil again, and put him off his stroke. He blew the drive out over the roadway on the left and lost any hope he might have had of catching Steve. Twenty pounds down the drain. Not a happy day.

"Want to get your money back tomorrow, Mr. Roberts?" asked a cocky Steve.

"O.K., nine o'clock," growled Willy ungraciously.

That evening in the Roberts's home, the three sons of the house joined Willy, Lorna, her mother and Steve for dinner. The talk was of the day's events.

"How did the golf go today, Dad?" enquired one son.

"Not too good."

"Heard it cost you a few bob, Dad," chimed in another to much laughter. Willy was not amused.

"How was the driving lesson, Lorna?" asked another brother innocently.

"Terrible," said Lorna, plainly indicating that she, too, was not amused. "That was one of the worst ideas Steve has ever had. I'd rather go to the dentist!" There was a pregnant silence.

"So it was your idea, Steve, my boy?" asked Willy casually.

"Uh, well," stuttered Steve, "it's just that I thought you'd be the best one to teach Lorna, as you get along so well."

"Indeed!" said Mrs. Roberts, giving knowing glances around the table.

"Aye, indeed," said Willy thoughtfully. He got up from the dining table and brought a bottle of wine back from the kitchen.

"A toast," said Willy, "to Steve's great win today."

Several toasts and three bottles of wine later, Willy insisted on bringing all the young men down to the local "for a nightcap" while the girls watched their favourite soap on TV. His sons were amazed at his uncharacteristic generosity in the bar. Fortunately for Steve, he lived within walking distance of the pub and just made it home before collapsing onto his bed and falling asleep without even changing into his pyjamas. He had a very restless night and was not in the best of health the next morning on the first tee.

Willy had little trouble getting his money back.

✌ The Big Dream ✌

————

OLLIE SAT IN the most comfortable armchair in the lounge, overlooking the eighteenth green. The sun was streaming in through the windows, warming his old bones. Members greeted him cordially as they came and went from the friendly room. He was partial to hot toddies at this time of the year, when the visitors had nearly all left Lahinch and an autumnal chill was in the air. He loved the bite of the Irish whiskey and the smell of the cloves as they released their pungent aroma. He relished the warm trickle of the golden liquid as it slipped down his throat and the pleasant glow that shortly afterward permeated his whole being.

"Ollie, Ollie, how are you keeping?" said Maxi Kavanagh as she entered the room and saw him in his favourite armchair by the window. Ollie beamed when he heard the friendly voice.

"Ah, Maxi, me auld flower, you're getting me all excited again, after the Doc telling me to take things easy."

They both laughed and she kissed him on the cheek. They chatted easily about mutual friends in the Lahinch and Ennistymon area for a few minutes and then Maxi ambled off to the ladies' locker room to change for her game.

Ollie took another sip of his hot toddy and relaxed in his big chair, thinking of all the lovely girls he had known in his 85 long years. A little tear came into his rheumy eyes as he dwelt on the memory of his beautiful Trish, the Pride of Doolin, his one true love and faithful wife of some 50 years. He saw her now as the young beauty he had married all those years ago, eyes sparkling, long dark hair blown by the wind, fair skin and perfect teeth. In his mind she was always laughing. Their courtship made his heart beat faster in recollection and the early passionate years of their marriage made him feel positively dizzy. He took another mouthful of his drink to steady himself. He was startled by a hand on his shoulder.

"Ollie, my good man, how are you this fine day?" It was the Captain.

"Mr. Captain, sir, I am very well indeed. And how are you," enquired Ollie, "in the autumn of your year of office?"

"Couldn't be better, Ollie. But, to be perfectly honest, I'll be glad to see the back of it. It's getting to be a very onerous task. Almost too much for one man. My wife and family will be glad to see a bit more of me next year. And the business could do with more time, too, I can tell you! But you'd know all that, having been both Captain and president yourself, way back when, wouldn't you, Ollie?"

"Ah, I don't think things were as demanding then. I can re-member that weeks would go by without me coming to the Club at all and the place would virtually run itself. I don't think you could do that now, with all the activities and staff to keep an eye on."

"No, indeed," said the Captain, getting up. "Can I freshen your drink, Ollie, before I go?"

"That's very kind of you, Captain. The Doc said I should ease back on the hard stuff, but, sure, what else is there nowadays?"

"Barman, another toddy for our distinguished member. Good luck, Ollie, and take care of yourself. Don't forget the card schools will be starting soon and they would not be the same without you."

Ollie waved as the genial Captain walked away and then settled back into his chair again, enjoying being in this place, in his Club, among his friends.

He tossed back the last of his drink as the barman brought out another steaming glass. His eyes were getting heavy and he felt a pleasant drowsiness coming over him. He gave in to it and drifted off into a gentle sleep. Soon he was dreaming. The dream was peopled with young men, many of whom he appeared to know. They were getting ready to play golf, amid much laughter and high spirits. The lads were going to play four-balls and they became a little more serious when they got down to the golf. Ollie himself started to play wonderfully, blasting drives down the middle and carving his irons left or right at will. His partner and opponents were also playing inspired golf and the game was very tight, never more than a hole in it all the way.

Coming to the third last hole one up, Ollie and his partner could wrap up the match with a win. It was a long par 3 over thick rough and Ollie's partner played first.

Duck hook! Over to Ollie.

In his dream, time seemed to stop and Ollie did everything in slow motion. He was acutely aware of all that he saw and did. The sun was actually hot on his skin. The shine off the nearby sea was blinding. The grass was never greener. He took out his 4-iron. He took the ball out of his pocket with a tee between his fingers, ready to insert into the turf. The ball was sparkling white and the tee was brilliant yellow. He could feel the tee sliding between the blades of grass and crunching into the sandy soil. He stood up slowly, took his stance and waggled his club back and forth in preparation. The shiny steel shaft glinted in the sun like flashes of lightning and the swishing of the club seemed to fill the air. He concentrated for all he was worth on the ball. He seemed to take an eternity to start the club moving back. Every muscle in his body tingled. Keeping his eye fiercely on the ball, he started the club down with his hips, which swept past the ball before his hands followed, pulling the club head into the back of the ball.

Then a strange thing happened. As the club struck the ball and it took off, he had the sensation of actually being the ball as it left the tee. He soared out over the dunes and felt a great rush of air on his face. As he gained height, he could see more and more of the course below him. Some seagulls were squawking nearby, and he smiled to himself and hoped they would not get in his way and deflect him from the green toward which he was headed. At the apex of his trajectory, he could see almost all of the course, several miles to seaward and the village of Liscannor nestling in the sunny bay to the northwest. Then, for some unaccountable reason, the ball started to descend toward the green but he did not! A slight panic gripped him. He watched the ball as it fell and saw it land a couple of yards short of the pin, bounce twice and come to a stop not more than a foot from the hole. A "gimme" and probably dormie two! He looked back toward the tee and saw his three companions waving to him. He waved back and slowly realised that he would not be going down to join them again. He soared higher and higher, until the links was only a speck in the distance.

"Has Ollie's drink gone cold?" enquired the head barman. The young assistant went over and touched the glass.

"Yes, sir. Shall I get him another?"

"No, son," said the head barman, looking closely at Ollie's pale, still figure. "I don't think he'll need it where he's going."